Mexico

& Central America

Mexico

& Central America

A Fiesta of Cultures, Crafts, and Activities for Ages 8–12

Mexico • Guatemala • Belize • El Salvador
Honduras • Nicaragua • Costa Rica • Panama

Mary C. Turck

CHICAGO REVIEW PRESS

Library of Congress Cataloging-in-Publication Data
Turck, Mary.
Mexico and Central America : a fiesta of culture, crafts, and activities for
ages 8-12 / by Mary C. Turck.— 1st ed.
      p. cm.
Includes bibliographical references and index.
ISBN 1-55652-525-7
1. Mexico—Social life and customs—Juvenile literature. 2. Central
America—Social life and customs—Juvenile literature. 3. Arts—Mexico—
Juvenile literature. 4. Arts—Central America—Juvenile literature. 5.
Handicraft—Mexico—Juvenile literature. 6. Handicraft—Central
America—Juvenile literature. I. Title.
F1210.T78 2004
972—dc22

                                                        2004003703

Dedication

To Mirna Anaya, Elvia Alvarado, and the people of
Mexico and Central America, whose lives have been
an inspiration and a challenge to me.

Published by Chicago Review Press, Incorporated
814 North Franklin Street
Chicago, Illinois 60610
ISBN 1-55652-525-7
Printed in the United States of America
5 4 3 2 1

Note from the Author

For as long as I can remember, I have wanted to know more about Latin America. In high school, I studied Spanish. When I grew older, I lived and worked in a Latino neighborhood in Chicago. In 1977 I visited Honduras with a friend who had served in the Peace Corps there. For the first time, I plunged into a country, culture, and language different from my own. Everywhere we went we were welcomed with courtesy and kindness.

During the 1980s, I met Central Americans as they visited Minnesota, where I live. Many of them were heroes, women and men whose courage was an inspiring example to me. They worked for peace and justice in their countries. They treasured the riches of their country's history and culture. Even when life looked grim, they found hope in the vision and work they shared.

I hope that this book will open a window to the exciting and fascinating countries of Mexico and Central America. My wish is that readers will find in *Mexico and Central America* reasons to go on learning about and from all of Latin America.

Contents

Acknowledgments

Thanks to my *compañera*, Nancy Black; to the Resource Center of the Americas; and especially to Teresa Ortiz, Rosita Balch, Irma Merfeld, Darla Baker, and Mary Swenson for their advice and encouragement.

Introduction

More than 130 million people live in the eight countries that make up Mexico and Central America. They speak Spanish, English, Garifuna, Tzotzil, and dozens of other Mayan languages. Farmers grow mangoes, bananas, coffee, beans, rice, corn, pineapples, trees, and other crops too numerous to list. People in cities work in factories, drive cabs, run hotels, and wait tables in restaurants. They paint, write poetry, cut paper into intricate patterns, embroider, and weave. They eat *tamales*, chocobananas, beans, sugarcane, and McDonald's hamburgers.

Organizing information about these wonderful cultures is a challenge, and trying to accomplish this in one book, while doing justice to the diversity and beauty of these cultures, is even more difficult. With this in mind, *Mexico and Central America: A Fiesta of Cultures, Crafts, and Activities for Ages 8–12* begins in the first chapter with a description of the Aztec and Maya roots shared by much of Mexico and Central America. Chapter 2 gives a brief introduction to each country, using maps and facts about each country's population and geography. Chapter 3 visits the mountainous highlands that run like a spine through Central America, and introduces Salvadoran painting and Honduran wood carving. Chapter 4 travels along the Atlantic Coast, where many of the communities share the riches of African culture and heritage, including the Garifuna music of the descendants of courageous Africans who escaped from a slave ship. Chapter 5 begins with Yini Carolina's journey to her Honduran school and includes stories of students and schools in other countries, as well as games and projects from those schools. Poetry and revolution, murals and clay mix in Chapter 6, as the art and literature of the region take center stage. Chapter 7 gets down to the serious business of daily work, whether that is raising corn and making tortillas or working in a factory and organizing a union. In Chapter 8, life-cycle celebrations include the rituals of birth in the Guatemalan highlands and the fifteenth-birthday celebrations of girls throughout Mexico and Central America. Activities include making *piñatas* and decorative *papel picado*. Chapter 9 turns from family celebrations to patriotic and religious holidays, from the fireworks of Nicaragua's *Gritería* to the candle-lit *luminarias* of a Mexican Christmas. The final chapter focuses on emigration to the United States, with stories of individual emigrants and a play presenting one journey.

Each chapter includes activities that you can do at home or in the classroom. Each chapter includes sidebars of information including some Spanish vocabulary. A resource guide at the end of the book includes recommended books, Web sites, and videos for further exploration; suggested places to enjoy more of the culture of Latin America in the United States; and a calendar of holidays and celebrations. The Teacher's Guide provides suggestions for teachers who want to use the activities in the classroom and identifies ages for various activities and suggests modifications.

Giant faces are among the many sculptures found on the pyramids and in the ancient ceremonial centers of the Maya.
Courtesy of Nancy Black and Mary C. Turck

Ancient Roots

Thirty-five hundred years ago, people in Mexico and Central America built cities. They explored science and experimented with art. Businesses sent salespeople and buyers on long trading journeys. Kings sent armies to conquer their neighbors.

This chapter introduces the Mayas, who built cities in Mexico, Guatemala, Belize, El Salvador, and Honduras as early as 1500 B.C.E. The Maya included great architects, astronomers, and mathematicians. This chapter introduces Maya math.

The Mayas were not alone. Other civilizations included the Olmec, Zapotec, Teotihuacán, Toltec, Mixtec, and Otomí. The Aztec people created one of the best-known civilizations. This chapter describes their floating gardens and calendar stones, as well as their conquest by the Spanish in 1519.

The Gregorian calendar, which is the one we use in everyday life, measures time from the birth of Jesus. Years before his birth are named "Before Christ" and counted backward—1 B.C. is a year closer to us than 2 B.C., 100 B.C. is 50 years closer to our time than 150 B.C., and so on. Similarly, years since the birth of Jesus are called A.D., which stands for the Latin words *anno Domini*, meaning "the year of our Lord."

Increasingly, scholars object to making the world's calendar a Christian calendar. Many use C.E., for the "Common Era" we now live in. They replace B.C. with B.C.E., meaning "Before the Common Era." This makes the terms religiously neutral and avoids offending non-Christians.

The Mayas

Deep in the rainforests of Central America, cities grew. Workers hauled giant stones. Astronomers measured directions of sun and stars and directed the placement of foundation stones. Slowly, giant pyramids rose above the trees. Artists carved jaguars out of stone. Priests supervised altars and secret passageways.

Smaller houses surrounded the central cities. Some cities grew larger than any in the world. But the rest of the world knew nothing of them, and the Mayas knew nothing of it. During the first millennium, the Mayas continued to build.

The Mayas combined science, religion, and government. A small number of people made up a noble class of priests and rulers. The pyramids and ball courts (used in ceremonial games, although the rules of the games are no longer known) played important religious roles. Astronomers also used the pyramids to track the movement of the moon and Venus. Physicians developed important herbal medicines.

Maps

Today's countries did not exist centuries ago. The Maya lived in what is now southern Mexico, Guatemala, Honduras, El Salvador, and Belize. In their time, none of these countries existed. This map shows some of the major cities of the Maya world (indicated by the square shape).

The Maya people developed a writing system. Scribes were trained to read, write, and use arithmetic. They recorded victories and the accomplishments of the king. They wrote down history and stories.

Scribes often accompanied important people on journeys. They helped keep records of trading. They also recorded any agreements reached. Scribes held an important and honored place in society.

In this activity, you'll work as a scribe. Your goal is to record the events of a single week. Select only important events to record. You can choose to focus on your family or on the world. Writing in your notebook with a pencil is the easiest way to record events. If you make a mistake, you can always erase and start over. In their time scribes did not use pencils. They used paint and brushes.

Materials

Notebook
Pencil or pen

1. Scribes often used symbols to represent people or events. Maya kings each had their own unique symbol. Begin by creating a symbol for yourself, your family, your teacher, your pet, and anyone or anything important in your life that might be a part of your week's record of events.
2. Record an event each day. Briefly write about an event and any important details. For example, you might write about a family trip to the movies or the first snow of the year. If you are focusing on the world, you might write about a hurricane or about the president of one country visiting another.
3. At the end of your week, review the events you recorded. Does each event still seem important now that the week is over? Are there other events that you didn't record and now seem more important? Imagine if your words were painted. Would you be able to change your record of events?

Sit down with a parent or other adult and share your week with them by using your record. Be sure to explain your system of symbols, too.

The long-lived Maya civilization began about 1500 B.C.E. and continues to the present day. For hundreds of years, the Maya prospered. Kings ruled from Copán, Chichen Itzá, Tikal, and other cities. (See the map on page 3 for the major cities.)

Farmers built terraces on steep hillsides. They raised corn, beans, and squash. Women patted tortillas and cooked beans over wood fires. They wove elaborate designs into cloth. Artists created fine jewelry from pearls and jade. They carved intricate scenes into stone and pieced jade into *mosaics*, decorations made up of small, inlaid pieces. Stone carvings often show kings and the symbols of their reigns.

Suddenly, about 900 C.E., the Maya left their cities and abandoned their pyramids. No one knows why. Anthropologists argue about the reasons. Some blame a drought or crop failure. Others think the failure came from bad leadership by a king. Some say the cities used up all the natural resources around them. Whatever the reason, the rainforests grew over the pyramids, hiding them

Maya Math

This is the Maya math system. The shell is used as a symbol for zero, a dot for one, and a bar for five. The Maya counted by twenties, as we count by tens. The number twenty is written as a dot with a shell (meaning zero) under it.

Twenty-one is a dot on top for twenty and a dot below for one.

Twenty times twenty is four hundred—write it with a dot above and two shells beneath.

Can you figure out the Maya numbers not labeled?

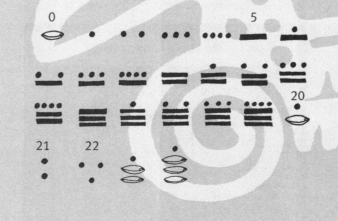

Embroidering Maya Designs

Traditional Maya fabrics identify people. Each town has its own designs. By looking at people's clothing, you can tell where they live. Designs can be woven right into the fabric or embroidered onto it.

In this activity you'll find instructions for how to embroider a square of cloth. You can then make this into the front panel of a pillow or sew it onto a book bag or backpack. You can also frame your embroidery and hang it on a bulletin board or give it as a gift. You can embroider Maya designs on the pockets of your favorite pair of jeans or add a Maya border to the hem of a skirt. Maya designs often incorporated animals, so you might choose to add this to your pattern, too.

Materials

Paper

Pencil

1 12-inch (30-cm) square of denim or sturdy
  cotton fabric

Washable fabric marker

Embroidery hoop

Embroidery floss, different colors (while you
  could embroider with regular sewing thread,
  embroidery floss works better because it is
  thicker and therefore more colorful)

Needles

1. Begin by planning your design and drawing some sketches. Zigzags make beautiful designs. They are sometimes called *cerritos*, meaning "little hills." They may also be a sign of the snake, which is a sky symbol. Or they may symbolize lightning, another sky sign.

Maya designs often repeat. You may choose to repeat a design over and over to make a border. For example, you might embroider the toad design. Toads represent rain, life, and fertility. Legend says that toads guard the cave of the rain god.

Here is a border made of toads:

Toads

Or you could combine several designs. A diamond design represents the earth, with the four corners for four directions. The smaller square in the center represents the sun. You might choose to embroider the outside of the diamond in shades of blue and the inside in a bright red or yellow. If you wanted to use traditional Maya colors, you would embroider the center in blue-green, the north in white, the east in red, the south in yellow, and the west in black.

Diamond

Crosses also represent the earth. They may represent the four directions. Sometimes people think of them as the world tree, with roots reaching deep into the earth and branches reaching for the sky.

Vulture

Cross

Jaguars or leopards

Choose one or more of the designs. You can repeat the same design or combine different designs.

2. Draw your design onto your fabric square with a pencil or washable fabric marker.
3. Place the fabric in the embroidery hoop.
4. Pick your floss colors.
5. Stitch away! If you have never embroidered before, here are a few tips:
   - The fabric is placed in a hoop to hold it tight and steady, which makes stitching the design easier.
   - Embroidery floss is made up of six strands. You can separate the strands and thread your needle with a single strand, or you can use a double or triple strand to sew a thick-

er line. A 12- to 18-inch (30- to 46-cm) length of thread is easiest to handle.
- When embroidering, people usually leave the thread unknotted. They catch the "tail" of the thread on the underside of the fabric in the first few stitches to keep it from unraveling.
- The easiest beginning stitch is called the *stem stitch*. Push your threaded needle up from the underside of the fabric to the top side. Leave a short "tail" of thread on the underside. Taking a small stitch (aim for six to eight stitches per inch), push the needle back through the fabric to the underside. For your next stitch, push the needle up so that it emerges on the topside in the middle of your first stitch. Then, move forward, with each stitch overlapping the previous one, so that they appear as a continuous line.
- Try to make your stitches short for the most attractive embroidery.

for nearly a thousand years.

Though the big cities and kings were gone, the Maya people continued to farm, weave, live, and die. For a thousand years, they lived in small villages. They made homes in mountains and forests. They kept alive their legends, art, and culture. Women wove symbols into the clothing they wore. Families passed down stories from generation to generation.

The Aztecs

Hundreds of years later, and far to the north, a wandering people began to build another great empire. The Aztecs were a *nomadic* people—that is, they wandered from place to place. Some of the Aztecs were also called the *Mexica*.

Eventually, the Aztecs settled in Mexico's central valley, where Mexico City is now located. They drove out the Olmec people, whom they found in the valley. The Aztecs searched for a place to build a city. Then, they saw a sign—an eagle, perched on a cac-

Flag of Mexico

Aztec Gods

The Aztecs had many gods. Each of the gods controlled some part of life, often some natural element:

Centeotl (sen-TAY-ohtl): the corn god

Ehecatl (ay-HAY-kahtl): the god of wind

Huitzilopochtli (hweet-see-lo-POHCH-tlee): the sun god, war god, guardian of Tenochtitlán

Mictlantecuhtle (meekt-lahn-tay-COOH-tlee): the god of the dead

Quetzalcoatl (ketz-ahl-KWAT-l): "Feather (quetzal) serpent"; the god of civilization and learning

Tezcatlipoca (tay-scaht-lee-POH-cah): the god of night

Tlaloc (tlah-lohk): the rain god

Tonatiuh (toh-nah-TEE-uh): the sun god, who is also the god of warriors

Tonantzin (toh-NAHN-tseen): "honored grandmother"

Xipe Totec (skee-pay-TOH-tec): the god of springtime and regrowth

Xiuhtecuhtle (ski-uh-tay-COOH-tlay): the fire god

Creating an Aztec Calendar

Artists labored for 52 years in order to carve and paint the Aztec Sun Stone, or Calendar Stone, from rock. The finished work is a giant stone circle measuring 12 feet (3.6 m) across and weighing about 27 tons (24 t). Based on even older Maya calculations, this stone shows a calendar that is more accurate and more than a century older than the Gregorian calendar we use today.

The Sun Stone has the sun's face in the middle, since the sun was the central Aztec god. The Aztecs believed that the earth was created and destroyed four times. They believed that they lived in the fifth creation. The stone's designs show the four previous eras of the earth as well as months and years. Two snakes circle the entire stone.

Materials

Large sheet of poster board or heavy paper
Pencil
Colored markers or paints
Paintbrushes (if using paints)
Ruler
Magazines
Photographs
Scissors
Glue

1. Begin with a large sheet of poster board or heavy paper. Use the pencil to sketch the largest circle possible. When you're satisfied with its size, trace over the pencil with a colored marker.
2. Draw a second circle, about two inches (five cm) smaller and inside the first. Trace over it with a marker.
3. Use your pencil to divide this inner circle into 12 equal parts. Each part will be one month of your year. To do this, use a ruler to draw a straight line from top to bottom across the center of the circle. Draw another line from left to right across the center of the circle. Divide each of the four sections you have made into three equal sections.

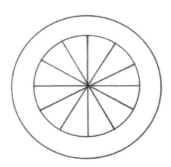

4. Decide on a different theme for each month. For example, February in Minnesota might feature skiing and snow. In Florida, you might choose to focus on valentines. Decide what each month means to you. You may choose more than one theme for each month. Be sure to remember to mark family celebrations—such as your birthday! Write the themes for the month in pencil on each of the 12 parts of your circle.
5. Look through magazines and photograph collections. Find photos, illustrations, or drawings to illustrate each theme. Cut these out (with permission when necessary). Arrange them in a collage that fills each month's space. When you have finished selecting and arranging these, glue them in place.
6. Complete your personal calendar by creating a border that shows important parts of your world. You might fill the border with family photos or with religious symbols—you decide.

Modeling a *Chinampa*

Twenty Days of the Aztec Month

Each Aztec month had 20 days. Each of the 20 days had a name. The names were:

Day 1 Cipactli (kee-PAHKT-lee): crocodile

Day 2 Ehecatl (ay-HAY-kahtl): wind

Day 3 Calli (cah-lee): house

Day 4 Cuetzpallin (kwets-PAHL-een): lizard

Day 5 Coatl (KWATL): serpent

Day 6 Miquiztli (mee-KWEEST-lee): death's head

Day 7 Mazatl (mah-zahtl): deer

Day 8 Tochtli (toch-tlee): rabbit

Day 9 Atl (AHTL): water

Day 10 Itzcuintli (eets-KWEEN-tlee): dog

Day 11 Ozomatli (oh-soh-MAHT-lee): monkey

Day 12 Malinalli (mah-lee-NAHL-lee): grass

Day 13 Acatl (ah-cahtl): reed

Day 14 Oceotl (oh-SEE-ohtl): ocelot

Day 15 Cuauhtli (kwah-OOHT-lee): eagle

Day 16 Cozcaquauhtli (cohs-cah-kwah-OOT-lee): motion

Day 17 Ollin (ohl-leen): flint

Day 18 Tecpatl (tayk-PAHT-l): rain

Day 19 Quiauitl (kwee-ah-OO-eetl): flower

Day 20 Xochitl (ski-OHCH-eetl): snake

Aztec *chinampas* were woven from reeds. Each giant mat of reeds was covered with mud or soil. Then, more layers of reeds and soil were added until the floating island was complete. Often willow trees were planted at the edge of the *chinampa* to hold it in place. Willows grow well in very wet places, and they grow very fast.

Once the *chinampa* was complete, food crops grew on it. A *chinampa* might hold corn, beans, and squash.

Materials

Cardboard

Acrylic paint, blue and brown

Paintbrushes

Translucent plastic, blue or clear

Glue

Craft foam, various colors

Scissors

Flexible drinking straws, thin

Yarn

1. Begin by painting a piece of display board so that the lake is blue. Let it dry completely.

2. Cut plastic to same size as the display board. Cover the lake with translucent plastic. Use the glue to affix this on three sides.

3. Add a few fish swimming here and there under the plastic by cutting them out of the colored foam and place underneath. Glue final side down.

4. Paint the straws brown and twist or weave them together braidlike to make a mat.

5. Cut plant shapes from the craft foam. Corn plants are tall, with long leaves. Bean plants are short, with round leaves. Squash plants crawl over the ground and sometimes climb up the cornstalks. A pumpkin is one kind of squash.

6. Cut strands of yarn and tie them to the bottom of each plant to make roots. Some of the roots can be woven among the reeds; some reach down to the bottom of the lake.

7. Place the plants on top of your mat, spreading them out. Glue some of the roots to the bottom of board under each plant so they hang out of the bottom. Glue plants in place if needed.

With your model *chinampa*, you can explain how the Aztecs built their floating gardens.

tus, holding a snake in its claw. About 1325 C.E., they built a great city on that site. They called it *Tenochtitlán* (tay-noch-teet-LAHN). Today, Mexico City is built over the ruins of Tenochtitlán.

The eagle holding a snake appears on the Mexican flag.

The Aztecs finished building Tenochtitlán in 1325 C.E. The grand city rose on five islands in a lake. Canals and bridges connected the islands. The Aztecs built *causeways* (raised highways), constructing them as narrow roads through the lake. An army could easily block the roads, defending the city against invaders.

Pyramids and castles rose above the island. Pyramids were used as religious temples. Castles were the homes of kings or royalty. A wall surrounded the grounds of the main temple. Inside, five hundred priests and their families lived, worked, sacrificed, and prayed to the gods.

The Aztecs also sacrificed to their gods. They declared war on neighboring peoples. Their weapons of war were wooden swords

Markets

Hernán Cortés, a Spanish military commander, described the markets of Tenochtitlán in a letter to King Charles V of Spain, written in 1520:

This city has many public squares, in which are situated the markets and other places for buying and selling. There is one square twice as large as that of the city of Salamanca, surrounded by porticoes, where are daily assembled more than sixty thousand souls, engaged in buying and selling; and where are found all kinds of merchandise that the world affords, embracing the necessaries of life, as for instance articles of food, as well as jewels of gold and silver, lead, brass, copper, tin, precious stones, bones, shells, snails, and feathers. . . .

Different kinds of cotton thread of all colors in skeins are exposed for sale in one quarter of the market, which has the appearance of the silk-market at Granada, although the former is supplied more abundantly. Painters' colors, as numerous as can be found in Spain, and as fine shades; deerskins dressed and undressed, dyed different colors; earthen-ware of a large size and excellent quality; large and small jars, jugs, pots, bricks, and endless variety of vessels, all made of fine clay, and all or most of them glazed and painted; maize or Indian corn, in the grain and in the form of bread, preferred in the grain for its flavor to that of the other islands and terra-firma; patés of birds and fish; great quantities of fish—fresh, salted, cooked and uncooked; the eggs of hens, geese, and of all the other birds I have mentioned, in great abundance, and cakes made of eggs; finally, everything that can be found throughout the whole country is sold in the markets.

Writing with Hieroglyphics and Making a Name for Yourself

Both the Aztec and the Maya wrote in hieroglyphics. That is, they used symbols, or *glyphs*, rather than an alphabet.

The Maya used about eight hundred glyphs that represented both ideas and sounds. A glyph might mean "hill" or "king" or "bird." Or it might be a sign for the sound "nee" or "sh." One glyph might have multiple meanings.

Maya scribes painted glyphs on accordion-folded books (*codices*). Sometimes glyphs were carved into altars or stone pillars called *stelae*.

The Aztecs used only picture glyphs. They had no glyphs for sounds, so they used similar-sounding words. For example, Mapachtepec (the name of a town) is written by drawing a hand (*maitl*) and a piece of moss (*pachtli*) on a hill (*tepec*). The glyphs for one word are put together in a single picture.

In this activity you'll discover how to write your name without an alphabet.

Materials

Paper
Pencils
Paint or markers
Paintbrushes (if using paint)

1. Begin by writing your name phonetically; that is, the way that it sounds. For example, if your name is Joseph, you might write: J—OH—SEH—F.
2. Choose pictures to represent the sounds in your name. In this example, Joseph might choose a jaguar for the "j" sound, an oak tree for the "oh" sound, and the number seven for the "sef" sound. That's "sev" instead of "sef"—close fits such as this, while not exactly correct, were often necessary.
3. Finally, figure out how to arrange your picture-glyphs together to make your name. The Aztecs usually wrote in vertical columns from top to bottom and then from the left side to the right side like this:

A   E
B   F
C   G
D   H

You would read this as ABCDEFGH, not as AEBFCGDH.

4. Draw your name with your picture glyphs and make it colorful. Aztec scribes and artists liked to use a lot of color.
5. Now think about the name you have just created for yourself. Do you like the hieroglyphs? Do they say anything about you? Try to create a second hieroglyphic name based on your interests, such as baseball, and your characteristics, such as curly hair.

Aztec Emperors

Aztec emperors ruled for nearly two hundred years. Moctezuma Xocoytl became emperor in 1502. He was the tenth Aztec emperor to rule from Tenochtitlán. Moctezuma became emperor, following his great-grandfather, father, and uncles to the throne.

Aztec emperors were chosen by a council of priests, warriors, and nobility. They usually chose an emperor's brothers to succeed him. If he had no brothers, then a son or nephew—one of the next generation of the royal family—would take his place. Like the Europeans, the Aztecs believed that the leader of the country had to be a man.

Moctezuma Xocoytl was the second emperor named Moctezuma. The first, his great-grandfather, ruled from 1440 to 1469. The older Moctezuma built botanical (plant) and zoological (animal) gardens, collecting every known species for study. He kept them in a zoo and enjoyed watching the animals from a balcony. The zoo survived until Cortés laid siege to the city in 1521. He ordered the zoo and all the animals burned, along with the rest of the city.

A great drought and famine weakened the empire. Axayácatl, the father of Moctezuma Xocoytl, reigned from 1469 to 1481. He reconquered territories that had rebelled during the dry times and put down rebellions.

After Axayácatl, his two brothers reigned until 1502.

with stone blades, bows and arrows, and spears. They wore padded suits of armor made of quilted cotton. They brought enemy captives home. Sometimes the enemies became slaves or family members. They were the lucky ones. Other captives were sacrificed to the Aztec gods. The Aztecs believed that some gods demanded human blood. For example, they believed that the sun god would die if he did not have human hearts to eat.

More than 200,000 people lived in Tenochtitlán, making it one of the largest cities in the entire world at that time. Every day, thousands of people came to the city's market squares. At the largest markets, the city's merchants bought and sold gold and silver as well as brightly colored cloth and food. Traders from distant places brought cotton, cocoa beans to make chocolate, and exotic bird feathers and animal skins. Sometimes cocoa beans were used as money.

Farmers raised food on giant floating gardens called *chinampas*. The *chinampas* were made of mats woven from reeds and

El Día de la Raza

Perhaps you know October 12 as Columbus Day, set aside to honor the sailing captain who "discovered" America. Christopher Columbus represents the conquest of Latin America by Europeans. Columbus and his crew treated the people they met very badly. Columbus is not very popular in Latin America. So a new holiday has developed.

October 12 is *El Día de la Raza*, meaning "The Day of the Race." This is a day celebrating the diverse peoples and cultures of the Americas. *El Día de la Raza* is observed throughout most of Mexico and Latin America.

Aztec Language

Some Aztec words became Spanish words, and some have become English words. *Chocolate* is an Aztec word that has also become a Spanish and English word. *Tomate* became a Spanish word—in English, we say *tomato*. *Chiquito*, an Aztec word meaning "small," became a Spanish word also meaning "small."

loaded with rich soil from the bottom of the lake. After years of planting, the mats sank lower in the shallow lake. Sometimes the roots of plants grew down through the *chinampas* and into the lake bed. Irrigated cornfields surrounded Lake Texcoco. Farmers also raised ducks, geese, and turkeys.

The great cities of the Maya and Aztec people disappeared, but the people did not. They continue to live in Mexico and Central America. Their contributions continue to enrich the world.

The people of Mexico and Central America are the descendants of the Aztec and Maya, but also of the Olmec and other people of the area as well as the Spanish invaders who arrived in 1519. In the next chapter, you will explore today's countries, with an overview of their modern boundaries and descriptions.

Learn a Little Spanish!

While the Maya still speak more than two dozen languages in Mexico and Central America, Spanish has become the common language of the area. In Spanish, words are usually pronounced just as they are spelled. The key to pronunciation is in the vowels:

A: "ah" sound, as in *mama*
E: long "a" sound, as in *day*; sometimes short "eh" sound, as in *ten*
I: long "e" sound, as in *sweet*
O: long "o" sound, as in *phone*
U: "oo" sound, as in *moon*
The double *l* is pronounced like a *y*.

usted (oos-TED) and se (SAY): you (polite, formal)
tu (TOO) and te (TAY): you (familiar, informal)
yo (YO): I
me (MAY): me
mi (MEE): my
el (ELL): he
ella (EY-ya): she
ellos, ellas (EY-yos, EY-yahs): they
nosotros (no-SO-tros): we

UNITED STATES

MEXICO

Gulf of Mexico

BELIZE

HONDURAS

GUATEMALA

NICARAGUA

EL SALVADOR

PANAMA

COSTA RICA

Mexico is actually part of North America. Central America lies between North America and South America.

2

Country by Country

While Mexico and the countries of Central America have a lot in common, each country has its own identity. For example, El Salvador takes pride in its many volcanoes. Nicaragua is a land of revolution. Costa Rica is proud that it has no army. This chapter looks at some basic facts about each of the countries.

Mexico

In the southern state of Chiapas (chee-AH-pahs), men and women work long hours growing corn and beans to eat. Children also help in the fields. These families living in southern Mexico are Maya Indians. They are descendants of the Mayas who built pyramids some 3,500 years ago.

The families carefully tend coffee plants. At harvest time, they will pick and sell the coffee beans. These farmers belong to a fair-trade cooperative, which pays a higher price for their beans than if these farmers sold their beans on the world market. Unfortunately, world coffee prices remain very low, and therefore so does the farmers' cash income.

After the work is done, adults attend a community meeting. The national government, they insist, does not respect Indians. They explain that's why they are poor and lack schools and medical care, and why they must organize themselves to improve their quality of life.

To the north, in Mexico City, tall office buildings reach for the skies and automobiles crowd the streets. This is the capital of Mexico and the seat of government. This city hums with activity. With more than 21 million people, it is either the second or third largest metropolitan area in the world. (Some sources say New York City is larger. Tokyo, with 31 million, is the largest.)

Farther to the north, factories spread over brown, parched land. Here, young women toil for 10, 12, and 14 hours a day. They sew blue jeans and shirts for sale in the United States. They earn less than a dollar an hour, but they are glad to have jobs. They have come from the rural southern states, such as Chiapas and Oaxaca (wah-HA-ka), where there are no jobs at all.

Mexico is a big country, almost three times as large as Texas. Only 10 countries in the world have more people than Mexico. With all its land and all its people, Mexico is a country of contrasts.

Population: 105 million

Area: 761,800 square miles (1,973,000 sq km; slightly less than three times the size of Texas)

Capital: Mexico City

Major language: Spanish

Natural resources: petroleum, silver, copper, gold, lead, zinc, natural gas, timber, and agriculture

Percent of population under the age of 14: 32.3 percent

Tijuana

Ensenada

Ciudad Juárez

Guaymas

Chihuahua

Nuevo Laredo

Matamoros

Topolobampo

Monterrey

La Paz

Durango

Mazatlan

León

Tampico

Guadalajara

Tuxpan

Cancún

Manzanillo

Mexico City

Campeche

Lázaro Cárdenas

Villahermosa

Acapulco

Oaxaca

San Cristóbal de las Casas

Belize

Warm skies, tropical breezes, sparkling beaches, colorful coral reefs—this looks more like the Caribbean than Central America. Indeed, Belize often seems more like the Caribbean islands than its Spanish-speaking neighbors. English is the national language, though Garifuna, Mayan languages, Spanish, and German are also spoken.

The histories of Belize's people are as varied as their languages. Some are Afro-Caribs or Garifuna, whose ancestors fought back and escaped from slave ships that had brought them from Africa to the Americas. The Atlantic Ocean near Central America is called the *Caribbean*. Much of the Atlantic Coast is considered the Caribbean Coast. Both of these names derive from an Indian group called the *Caribs*, who existed at the time of Columbus's landing and were then wiped out by the Spanish invaders. Some are Maya Indians, whose ancestors built spectacular pyramids. German Mennonites came over and formed competing communities. England colonized Belize, calling it British Honduras and establishing a British government in 1854.

Belize is the youngest and smallest country in Central America. After independence in 1981, it remained a member of the British Commonwealth. While Belize now governs itself, it still recognizes the queen (or king) of England as its head of state. (Many former British colonies keep this kind of relationship with Britain.)

Population: 266,000

Area: 8,900 square miles (23,000 sq km; slightly smaller than Massachusetts)

Capital: Belmopan

Major languages: English (official), Spanish, Mayan, Garifuna, and Creole

Natural resources: agriculture, timber, fish, and hydropower (creating electricity using waterpower)

Percent of population under the age of 14: 41.1 percent

What's in a Name?

What does it mean to be an American? Many people who live in the United States say they are Americans. Actually, everyone who lives in North or South America is an American. Canadians live in America. Mexicans live in America. Nicaraguans live in America. So do Brazilians, Colombians, and—you get the picture.

In Spanish, the United States is not called *America*. It is called *los Estados Unidos* (lose ess-TAH-dose oo-NEE-dose)—the United States. People who live in the United States of America are called *estados unidenses* (ess-TAH-dose oo-nee-DEN-sase).

Costa Rica

"*¡Un aplauso! ¡Un aplauso!*" ("Applause! Applause!") shouted the enthusiastic master of ceremonies. Bleachers filled with enthusiastic Costa Ricans responded with happy roars. In December 1987 President Oscar Arias returned to them, bearing the Nobel Peace Prize he won for his work for peace in Central America. His leadership in negotiations helped end civil wars in Nicaragua and El Salvador.

Costa Ricans took personal and national pride in the Nobel Peace Prize. Now the whole world recognized their democratic, peaceful country. Over and over, Costa Ricans told visitors the story of their success. It began, Costa Ricans said, when they abolished the army in 1949. Throughout Latin America, armies had often overthrown democratic governments. Costa Ricans decided to eliminate the threat. Since then, Costa Rica has not had an army. Costa Ricans maintain that this is the reason their country is the most peaceful, most prosperous, and most democratic country in all of Central America.

Population: 3.9 million
Area: 19,700 square miles (51,000 sq km;
    slightly smaller than West Virginia)
Capital: San José
Major languages: Spanish (official) and English
Natural resources: agriculture and hydropower
Percent of population under the age of 14:
    30.1 percent

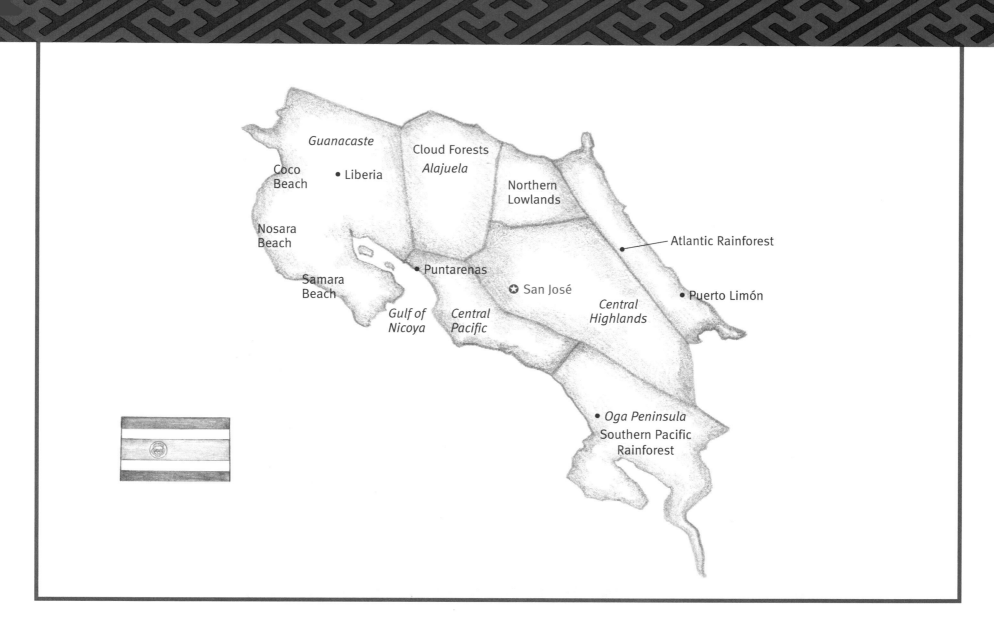

Guanacaste

Coco Beach

• Liberia

Cloud Forests

Alajuela

Northern Lowlands

Atlantic Rainforest

Nosara Beach

Samara Beach

• Puntarenas

Gulf of Nicoya

Central Pacific

✪ San José

Central Highlands

• Puerto Limón

• Oga Peninsula

Southern Pacific Rainforest

El Salvador

The "Land of Volcanoes" boasts more than 25 extinct volcanoes. (Some of these volcanoes are indicated on the map on the next page by a triangle shape.) Their forested cones rise among the mountain ranges of tiny El Salvador. Long after their fires dimmed, El Salvador continued to suffer from bloody political explosions.

During the 1970s and '80s, *guerrillas* (people engaging in irregular warfare) fought against military dictatorships. Government-affiliated death squads targeted union leaders, priests and nuns, and anyone they saw as "leftist," or against the government. More than 75,000 people died in the fighting, and 300,000 fled the country.

The war ended in 1992. Since then, the country has enjoyed a democratic and mostly peaceful government.

El Salvador is the most densely populated country in Central America. Its population is almost as large as Honduras, but its land area is less than one-fifth the size of Honduras. It is also a very industrialized country.

Poverty remains a major problem. The war left the country devastated. Then, in 1998, Hurricane Mitch swept through, creating more damage. In 2001 earthquakes struck, killing 1,200 people and leaving more than a million homeless. Today, the people of El Salvador are working to rebuild.

Population: 6.5 million
Area: 8,100 square miles (21,000 sq km; slightly smaller than Massachusetts)
Capital: San Salvador
Major language: Spanish
Natural resources: agriculture, timber, fish, and hydropower
Percent of population under the age of 14: 41.1 percent

Guatemala

Guatemala is the land of the Maya. From colorful, traditional clothing to more than 21 languages, the Maya people create a rainbow of nations within a single country. Traditional Maya clothing uses distinctive patterns to identify the home community of the wearer. During the brutal civil war of the 1970s, '80s, and '90s, the army targeted Mayas for repression and death. Many gave up their traditional clothing, hoping to escape notice.

More than 30 volcanoes rise as high as two miles (more than three km) above sea level. Mountain ranges cover much of the country. The Pacific Coast and El Petén's central jungle area offer fertile ground for banana plantations. Farmers grow coffee on the mountainsides. They also grow beans and corn to feed their families.

Guatemala still has a small number of very wealthy people who own most of the land and most of the businesses. The country also has a small middle class. However, most Guatemalans live in extreme poverty.

High unemployment means they cannot find jobs, so they lack money to pay for food and housing. They also suffer from government corruption, which prevents money from going to pay for schools, health care, and other public services, and from continuing threats to human-rights workers, journalists, and union activists.

Population: 13.9 million

Area: 42,100 square miles (109,000 sq km; slightly smaller than Tennessee)

Capital: Guatemala City

Major languages: Spanish, more than 21 indigenous languages. Guatemala's many Maya groups speak their own languages and preserve their own culture.

Natural resources: petroleum, nickel, rare woods, fish, chicle (used in chewing gum), and hydropower

Percent of population under the age of 14: 42.9 percent

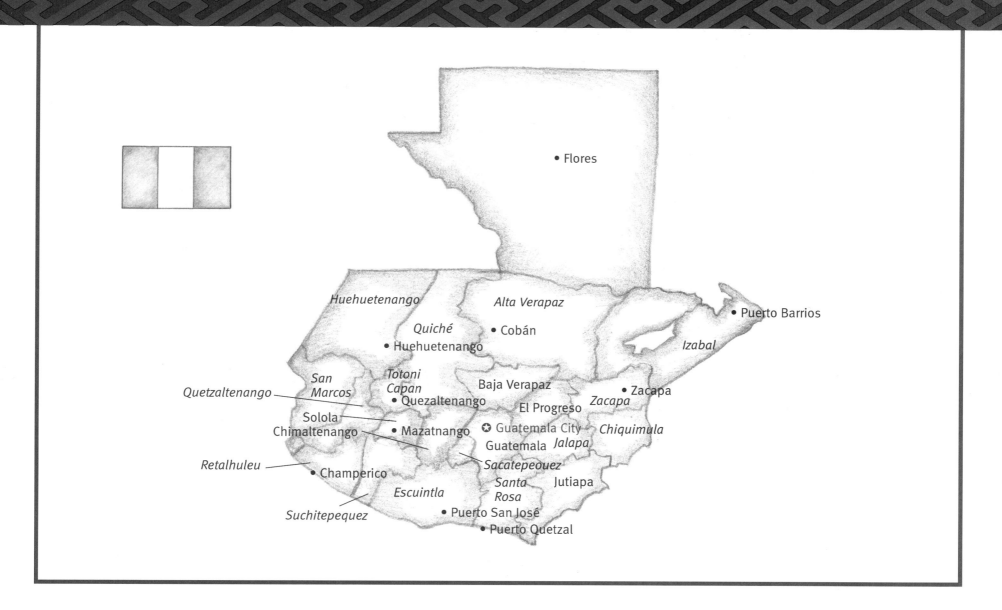

Flores

Puerto Barrios

Huehuetenango

Alta Verapaz

Quiché

Cobán

Huehuetenango

Izabal

San
Marcos

Totoni
Capan

Baja Verapaz

Zacapa

Quetzaltenango

Quezaltenango

Zacapa

Solola

El Progreso

Chimaltenango

Mazatnango

✪ Guatemala City

Chiquimula

Guatemala

Jalapa

Retalhuleu

Sacatepeouez

Champerico

Santa
Rosa

Jutiapa

Escuintla

Suchitepequez

Puerto San José

Puerto Quetzal

Honduras

A 10-year-old boy trudges up a mountainous country road. The razor-sharp *machete* (long, all-purpose knife) he carries is a farmer's tool. He's proud to be old enough and strong enough to own one. He carries it everywhere with him. Like the young boy, grown men walking and bicycling on the road also carry personal machetes.

Honduras is the most rural country of Central America, with more than half of its people still living in the countryside. A Honduran boy in the *campo* (countryside) grows up watching men use their machetes, the all-purpose tool of Central America. To a visitor, the razor-sharp machete looks like a dangerous weapon. To a Honduran farm worker, or *campesino*, the machete is simply another tool, an extension of his arm. With a machete, you can chop a tree or peel an orange or cut grass. For centuries, every boy has learned to use and respect this all-purpose knife.

Girls and boys, men and women have traditionally been assigned strictly separate roles in life, especially in the countryside. As in many other parts of the world, these roles have begun to change in recent years. Like her mother and grandmother, today's rural Honduran girl still works in the fields and cooks in the house. Unlike her mother and grandmother, however, she may also have and use her own machete. Today, she and her brother may both move to cities to escape the poverty of the countryside. Both boys and girls face new challenges, in cities and in the countryside.

Population: 6.7 million

Area: 43,200 square miles (112,000 sq km; slightly larger than Tennessee)

Capital: Tegucigalpa

Major languages: Spanish, indigenous languages, English

Natural resources: agriculture, timber, gold, silver, copper, lead, zinc, iron ore, antimony, coal, fish, and hydropower

Percent of population under the age of 14: 41.6 percent

Bay Islands

Tela
Puerto Cortés
San Pedro Sula
Cortés
Santa Barbara
El Florido
Copán
Santa Rosa De Copán
Agua Caliente
Anguiatú • El Poy
Lempira
Intíbuca
La Paz
Atlantida
La Geiba
Olanchito
Yoro
Comayagua
Comayagua
Francisco Morazan
La Esperanza
Tegucigalpa
Danlí
Las Manos
El Espino
El Amatillo
Valle • San Lorenzo
Ampala
El Tigre Volcano
Choluteca
Guasaule

Trujillo
Togoa
Colón
Limón • Palagios
Río Platano

Gracias a dios
Puerto Lempira

Olancho
Catacamas
Juticalpa
Río Coco
El Paraíso
Leimus

Nicaragua

In 1998 Hurricane Mitch stormed across Central America. The two thousand people living on the slopes of Posoltega Volcano were among its victims. As the hurricane's heavy rains filled the volcano's crater, the walls began to collapse. Giant mud slides buried and killed most of the residents.

Those who survived did not give up. With Nicaraguan determination, some three hundred families moved to the outskirts of the city of León. They formed a new community, Villa Soberana, and began to rebuild their lives.

Nicaraguans have had to rebuild their lives, their communities, and their country more than once. A revolution unseated a brutal dictator in 1979. (A *dictator* rules a country in the way he chooses, without listening to the people or holding elections.) Soon after, the country voted for the Sandinista revolutionaries to form a new government. The Sandinistas took their name from a long-ago Nicaraguan hero, Augusto Sandino, who fought against U.S. military occupation of the country. They fought to get rid of the dictatorship and to redistribute the country's wealth more equally. Another war soon began, with armies funded by the United States trying to overthrow the Sandinistas. The United States was afraid that the Sandinistas would be friends with Russia and Cuba, who were the United States' enemies at the time. Eventually, the Sandinistas were voted out of office, though they remain a major political party.

Wars, hurricanes, volcanoes, and earthquakes have left a legacy of poverty. Despite the hardships they face, Nicaraguans keep on rebuilding.

Population: 5.1 million

Area: 49,800 square miles (129,000 sq km; slightly smaller than the state of New York)

Capital: Managua

Major languages: Spanish, English, and indigenous languages

Natural resources: agriculture, gold, silver, copper, tungsten, lead, zinc, timber, and fish

Percent of population under the age of 14: 37.7 percent

Puerto Cabezas • Cayos Miskitos

Estelí •

Matagalpa •

Corinto •

León •

Puerto Sandino •

Lago de Managua

Managua

Rama •

Bluefields • • El Bluff

Granada •

Islas del Maíz

Lago de Nicaragua

Rivas •

San Juan del Sur • • San Carlos

Panama

On board the ship, the crew waits patiently. First, they have to process papers for immigration, permission to enter the canal, safety checks—the list seems to go on forever. Finally, the ship is cleared to enter the canal. The next available time is seven o'clock the following morning. They get a good night's sleep.

The next day, the yacht follows the same route used by giant ocean liners. Each ship enters a lock. (The *lock* is a large concrete box.) Water is pumped in to raise the water level (and the ship) 30 feet (9 m) higher. The pumps move more than 3,200,000 cubic feet (91,000,000 l or 91,000 kl) (90,700 t) of water in 15 minutes. When the ship is high enough, a gate opens, and it moves into the next lock.

The Panama Canal is a huge part of Panama's national identity. The United States helped Panama become a separate country from Colombia in 1903. Then, Panama and the United States signed a treaty so that the United States could build the canal and control the Panama Canal Zone. Panamanians grew to resent United States control of a part of their country. Like people in the United States or any other country, Panamanians wanted to run their own country without foreign interference. The United States finally returned the canal and canal zone to Panama in 1999.

Population: 3 million
Area: 30,100 square miles (78,000 sq km; slightly smaller than South Carolina)
Capital: Panama City
Major languages: Spanish and English
Natural resources: copper, mahogany forests, shrimp, and hydropower
Percent of population under the age of 14: 30.6 percent

Chapter 1 looked at the history of Mexico and Central America. Chapter 2 explored the individual countries, their geography, and a few things that make each one unique. In the next chapter, you will look at the mountainous highlands and the people who live there.

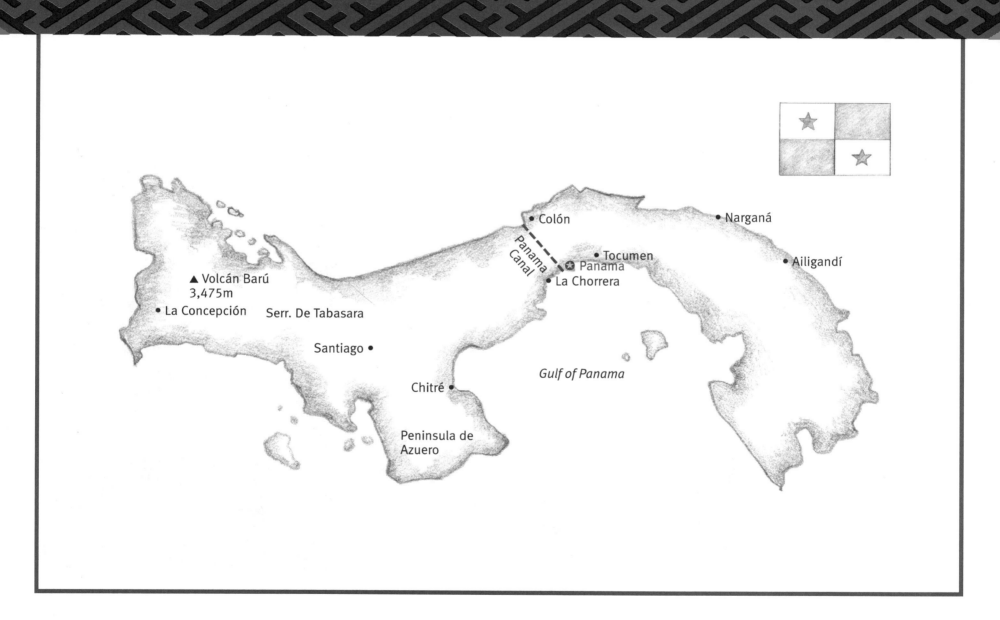

Volcán Barú
3,475m

La Concepción

Serr. De Tabasara

Santiago

Chitré

Peninsula de
Azuero

Colón

Panama
Canal

Tocumen

Panama

La Chorrera

Gulf of Panama

Narganá

Ailigandí

The view from Lemoa, Guatemala, looks out over mountains, valleys, and fields. Lemoa is in Guatemala's mountainous central highlands. *Courtesy of Nancy Black and Mary C. Turck*

3

Life Above the Clouds

"**F**asten your seatbelts for landing," the pilot announces. The plane begins a steep descent. Looking out the airplane window, you see trees and jungle rising above the plane. Are you going to crash into a mountain? The plane is still falling rapidly. As the wheels touch the ground, you finally breathe again. Welcome to the ups and downs of life in Central America!

Hurricane Mitch

Hurricane Mitch hit the northern coast of Honduras at the end of October 1998. After sweeping the country with winds up to 200 miles (about 320 km) per hour, the giant weather system sat there for six days, dumping rain on the land day after day. Some parts of the country received more than four feet (over one m) of rain in less than a week!

Hurricane Mitch's rains triggered floods and mud slides. With mountainsides bare from previous deforestation, mud rushed down the slopes. Floodwaters washed away everything in their path. At least 15 villages were totally destroyed. Dozens of bridges and roads were washed away, leaving parts of the country entirely isolated.

More than ten thousand Hondurans died as a result of Hurricane Mitch. More than a quarter of a million homes were destroyed, and about a million people were driven from their wind- and water-damaged homes. Churches throughout the country were turned into shelters for homeless hurricane refugees.

This chapter tells about life in the mountain highlands. Mountain nights can be cold, so you can make a poncho like those worn in the highlands. You can also build a volcano, like those that still grumble and occasionally erupt in the mountains, and read an Aztec story about two Mexican volcanoes.

A spine of mountains runs from Mexico through Central America. On the northeast side of the mountains, the Atlantic Coast lowlands are hot, humid, and wet. On the southwest side of the mountains, the Pacific lowlands are generally hotter and drier. The mountainous highlands have more moderate climates.

Mountains surround the airport in Tegucigalpa (tah-goo-see-GAHL-pa), Honduras. Mountains cover most of Central America. They surround the central plateau in Mexico. The highest reach 14,000 feet (4,700 m).

In Honduras, a paved road winds through the mountains up to the town of La

Libertad (la lee-bare-TAHD) in the central part of Honduras, near the city of Comayagua (ko-my-AH-gwah). Rain has washed out chunks of the road. Here and there, signs warn of falling rocks. In some places, rocks have fallen from the mountain, blocking part of the road. A giant pothole looks large enough to lose a pig in. Auto traffic is not heavy.

Most rural Hondurans walk. They cannot afford to buy cars. *Burros* (donkeys) are a more common form of transportation. The sturdy little animals live on grass and carry people or loads of wood or vegetables to the market. People who have a little more money may ride horses. Bicyclists with wiry muscles carry machetes, baskets, sacks, and sometimes even a passenger or two. Buses grind slowly up the mountain in low gear, stopping to pick up passengers wherever they appear. Buses, bicycles, and burros share the road with people. Men walk, carrying machetes to their fields or firewood to their homes. Women carry children, buckets of water, or both. Students walk to school.

Living in the Mountains

The small city of La Libertad perches on the side of a mountain in Honduras. People in town live in *adobe* (a-DO-bee) houses, or houses made of mud bricks. Walls may be 1 foot (30 cm) thick. The thick walls help to keep the summer heat out.

Many people here build their own homes. First, they build forms to shape the bricks. Then, they mix soil and water and pack it tightly into the forms. When the bricks are dry, they are removed from the forms. Then the bricks sit in the sun to "cure" for days, so they will be hard and long lasting. Finally, the bricks are stacked to make the walls of a house.

A typical city home in La Libertad has electric lights and a wood cook stove. Water comes from a pump in the backyard. The

Carving

Wood carving produces both useful and beautiful objects. Wheelbarrows bump along on carved wooden wheels. Carved wooden bowls hold food. Little children play with wooden toys carved by *Papá* (Dad) or *Abuelo* (a-BWAY-lo) (Grandpa).

Wooden cats with long tails come from Oaxaca in Mexico. In Honduras, a coin is part of each decorative wooden bowl. Artists carve faces of ancient Maya gods. Some carvers polish their work to a high gloss. Others paint wooden statues.

While carving hard woods takes a lot of time and practice, soap carving is pretty easy. And you can produce some beautiful work!

Materials

Bar soap, bath size

Tracing paper

Pencil

Scissors

Craft sticks

Toothpicks (optional)

Paper plate

Acrylic paints, bright colors

Paintbrushes

1. Start with a large bar of soap. Choose a simple design to carve into it, such as a fish or a sun.

2. First make a pattern for your soap carving on a piece of paper. You may trace a design from a book or other source, or you may draw one freehand. To make a simple fish, begin by drawing an oval shape. Add a triangle for the tail and a circle for the eye. Now, draw a small mouth. And, there—you have a fish!

3. After you have traced or drawn your pattern, cut it out and place it on top of the bar of soap.

4. Use a craft stick to trace around the edges of the pattern, making an impression of this design on the bar of soap. Remove the pattern. Use the craft stick to make a deeper impression and chip away at the soap around the basic pattern.

5. Now that your basic pattern is carved, you can begin to carve details. Use another craft stick or a toothpick. For the fish, shape the body so that it has no sharp edges. Carve scales, gills, and an eye (or eyes if front view). Use the pattern as a guide—but use your own imagination to make a unique carving!

6. When you are finished, you can paint your carving. Experiment with making different colors by combining paints. Put a small amount of blue on a paper plate. Add a bit of white and mix them together. Do you like this shade? What will happen if you add some yellow to the mixture? Try bright colors—don't worry about whether you are mixing realistic colors (although there really are amazing color combinations of fish). You might want a red sun or a purple fish.

Learn a Little Spanish!

día, días (DEE-ah, DEE-ahs): day, days

muerto (MWEHR-toh): dead

vivo (VEE-voh): alive

invierno (een-vee-AIR-noh): winter

primavera (PREE-ma-VAY-rah): spring

verano (veh-RAH-no): summer

otoño (oh-TOH-nyoh): autumn

arbol (AHR-bohl): tree

flor (FLOHR): flower

bosque (BOH-skay): forest

lluvia (YOU-vee-ah): rain

nube (NOO-bay): cloud

sol (SOHL): sun

outhouse is also there. The house may have two or three small rooms and dirt floors. Sweeping every day keeps the floors hard, smooth, and clean.

In the rural areas around La Libertad, families live on farms or in small villages. Their homes usually do not have electricity. People in the rural areas grow their own food. Everyone helps. All the farm work is done by hand. Every child old enough to hold a hoe works in the garden or fields. Children watch the family cow as it looks for grass to eat. They may gather wood or haul water from a river or well. Everyone works to feed the family.

The climate changes with the altitude in Central America. Temperature varies more from high altitudes to low altitudes than it does from December to July. On the Atlantic and Pacific coasts, the sun bakes sandy beaches. Bananas and pineapples grow in tropical heat. Driving along the coastal highway, you can smell the pineapples from roadside stands. Bananas grow in dozens of varieties—long, short, green, yellow, red.

Coconuts are everywhere. Higher in the mountains, the temperature drops. Here, farmers grow corn and beans on steep hillsides. They tend coffee bushes that grow in small plots, often shaded by larger trees.

Saving the Forests

Forests once covered most of Central America. Now, nearly two-thirds are gone. Almost 1,000,000 acres (405,000 ha) are *deforested* (cut down or destroyed) each year. Some forests are cut for their beautiful mahogany and rosewood trees. Some are cleared to make room for farming and cattle ranching. Farmers raise food to feed their families, and sometimes to sell to other people. Cattle ranchers sell the cattle, often to restaurants and food processors in other countries. Some wood is cut down to use in cooking fires.

Forestland is not good for farming. The land often lacks the nutrients that crops need. Trees and other plants hold the soil in place on mountainsides. Trees shelter the soil

Sewing a Poncho

High in the mountains, nights can be chilly. *Serapes* (ponchos), which are heavy wool blankets, protect against the mountain cold. Women spin and weave woolen fabric from sheep's wool. They may dye the yarn in bright colors. You, too, can make a poncho!

Materials

1½ yards (2 m) of wool, fleece, or other
    medium to heavy fabric
Ruler
Marker
Scissors
Ribbon or braid
Pins
Needle
Thread
Sewing machine (helpful, but not necessary)

1. Fold the fabric in half lengthwise. Then, fold it in half in the other direction. The corner where all the folds meet is the exact center of the fabric.
2. Measure 4 inches (10 cm) out from this point in four directions. Using a marker, connect these four points forming a box.

3. Cut out this square.
4. Try on your poncho. Hold your arms out straight. Is the poncho too wide for you? It should reach your wrists when you hold your arms out straight from your shoulders. If it reaches past your wrists, you will need to make it smaller. Have someone help you to measure and decide how much fabric to cut off. Cut the same amount from each side.

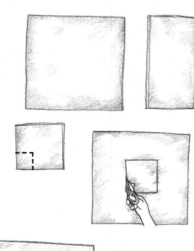

5. Wrap the neck edges carefully with the ribbon or braid. This will keep the neck hole from fraying. You want a "sandwich," with the ribbon or braid taking the place of the bread, while the neck edge is the filling. Be sure you have covered all the cut edges of the fabric with the ribbon or braid. Pin it securely in place. Carefully sew the three layers of the "sandwich" together.

6. Hem the outer edges of your poncho. Turn the edges under about half an inch (1.3 cm) and sew them. Or you can cover all the edges with ribbon or braid. Be sure to hem or cover the edges on both sides and on the top and bottom.
7. If you like, you can also embroider designs on your poncho or sew on ribbons in colorful patterns. (See Embroidering Maya Designs in Chapter 1, on page 7, if you want to embroider some traditional designs.)

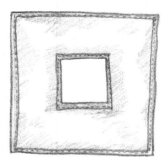

Volcano Stories

An ancient Aztec story tells of Popocateptl (po-po-kah-TAY-petl) and Iztaccihuatl (ees-tah-SEE-watl). Popocateptl (known as "Popo") was an Aztec warrior. His name means "smoking mountain." He loved the beautiful Iztaccihuatl (known as "Itza"), whose name means "white woman." Her father disapproved of their love. While Popo was away, Itza's father told her that Popo had been killed in battle. The grieving Itza killed herself.

When Popo returned and learned of her death, he built a great mound and buried her in it. This mound is the sleeping volcano, Iztaccihuatl. Then, Popo vowed that he would never leave her. He killed himself and he, too, became a volcano. Today, his burial mound still stands next to her. Popocateptl is a living volcano, forever holding a torch aloft at the foot of his true love.

Manlio Argueta, a famous writer from El Salvador, has written another volcano story entitled *Magic Dogs of the Volcanoes*. This is the tale of two ancient volcanoes that help magical dogs protect the people from soldiers.

from wind and rain. Low-growing shrubs and grasses help, too. When mountain forests are cut, rains wash away the soil and the wind blows it away. This is called *erosion*.

When fields are cultivated to grow crops, the soil is easily eroded even faster. Cultivating fields means digging up and turning over the soil. Digging exposes the soil to wind and rain. The top layer of soil is the most fertile soil. When the most fertile soil is eroded away, crops will no longer grow.

On mountainsides, heavy rain can also cause landslides and floods. Livestock, homes, and even people are swept away in the floods and landslides.

Other forests have been cut to make room for cattle. When cattle graze on mountainsides, the land degrades quickly. Soon it is not even good for pasture. People in Honduras say, "The cattle are eating the mountains."

In Costa Rica, misty, mysterious cloud forests cover high mountain slopes. (A *cloud forest* is a special type of rain forest. A *rain forest* is a tropical woodland that receives at least 100 inches [254 cm] in annual rainfall.) Bathed in clouds, the high forests abound in ferns, mosses, and orchids. About 450 different types of orchids grow in the Monteverde cloud forest in Costa Rica. Because Monteverde is so high, its average temperature is only 65°F (18°C).

In Honduras, La Tigra National Park houses a large wildlife preserve. Honduran wildlife includes deer, monkeys, wild boars, peccaries, tapirs, badgers, coyotes, wolves, foxes, jaguars, pumas, black panthers, alligators, iguanas, coatis, sloths, armadillos, and more than seven hundred species of birds! Many animals such as the jaguar, the largest New World cat, have become rare because of over-hunting. In La Tigra, moss, ferns, and dense trees shelter wildlife in a cloud forest at the top of El Picacho Mountain.

Throughout Central America, people struggle to preserve the forests. Costa Rica, for example, has officially protected about 12 percent of its land area. Several projects in Guatemala plant trees to reforest land. Small farmers raise shade-grown coffee, which thrives under a forest canopy. Organic farming methods preserve the rich diversity of rainforest life. (*Organic* means that farmers do not use pesticides or chemical fertilizers.)

Another Kind of Mountain

Volcanoes make up many of the mountains of Mexico and Central America. Some of the volcanoes are still active. The Cerro Negro (SEHR-oh NEG-roh) Volcano near León, Nicaragua, erupts from time to time, pouring ash over the city and countryside. After 20 years of quiet, the volcano became quite active again in 1992, covering León with clouds of ash and causing at least $20 million in damage to homes and crops. An eruption in 1995 sent lava flows almost 1 mile (1.6 km) down its slopes and drove more than a thousand people from their homes. Earthquakes often accompany eruptions. The volcano also belches clouds of ash, dumping tons of ash on nearby communities. During an eruption, the clouds of ash block the sunlight. Over time, volcanic

ash can help make rich farmland. But, when it first falls, ash destroys crops and pollutes the air.

While El Salvador is known as the "Land of Volcanoes," these unpredictable giants spread from Mexico through Central America. Every country of Central America, except for tiny Belize, has volcanoes.

Los Días de los Muertos

In the mountains, life and death exist side by side. In early November, the living celebrate the dead with the holiday *Los Días de los Muertos* (The Days of the Dead). On this day, people remember parents and children who have died. They recall grandparents and aunts and uncles. They honor the dead especially at this time of year.

The Days of the Dead are a special holiday in Mexico and Central America. Stores offer special toys and sugar candies shaped like skeletons or skulls. People may decorate little altars (*ofrendas*) in their homes. (See Chapter 6 for the "Creating an *Ofrenda*" activity.)

People go to cemeteries to decorate the graves of family members. Sometimes they bring a picnic to enjoy at the graveside. They may also bring the dead person's favorite food. After all, the dead people are not scary strangers. They are Grandma and Grandpa, Cousin Jacinta, Uncle Jorge. The dead are friends and family. It is good to take time to remember them.

Painting in the Salvadoran Style

In El Salvador, paintings burst with the color and life of the natural world. Simple shapes represent homes, birds, corn, flowers, sun, and mountains. Every color is bright and clear. In this activity you will make a bookmark using the style of Salvadoran artists.

Materials

Cardstock
Ruler
Scissors
 Pencil
Carbon paper
Paper clips
Acrylic paints, bright colors
Paintbrushes, various widths, including one
    with a very fine tip

1. To make a bookmark, begin by cutting out a piece of cardstock that is 2 by 6 inches (5 by 15 cm).
2. Use carbon paper to trace one of the simple designs below onto the cardstock. Place the carbon paper between the page and the card- stock. Make sure that the dark, coated side of the carbon paper is facing the cardstock. Use paper clips to attach the three sheets (book page, carbon paper, cardstock) so they do not shift position. Then, use a pencil or other pointed object to trace along the lines of the design. The carbon paper will transfer the design to the cardstock.
3. Paint in the design, using bright, cheerful col- ors. Traditional Salvadoran paintings use con- trasting colors side by side. For example, the bird's body might be bright yellow and the tail feathers might be green and blue.
4. To create your own Salvadoran-style design, use the graphics as patterns or to give you ideas. Layer one design on top of another. For exam- ple, you might begin with a house, then put a tree in front of the house and a bird on the tree. Let each layer dry before painting the next so that the colors do not mix. Fill every space on the cardstock. Experiment and have fun!

Blowing Off Steam

Would you like to astonish your friends? Frighten your relatives? It's easy! Just make your own volcano and watch it erupt over and over at your command.

Materials

Adult assistance suggested
Newspapers
Cardboard box, at least 15 inches (38 cm) square
Pencil
Ruler
Scissors
Aluminum foil
Mixing bowl
Measuring cups
Measuring spoons
6 cups (1.4 l) flour
2 cups (500 ml) salt
4 tablespoons (60 ml) cooking oil
2 cups (500 ml) warm water
Food coloring, brown, green, and red
16 ounce (500 ml) plastic soda bottle, empty
Funnel
1½ cups (375 ml) water

10 drops liquid dish detergent
2 tablespoons (30 ml) baking soda
½ cup (125 ml) vinegar

1. Cover a table with several layers of newspaper. Place the cardboard box on the newspaper. Draw a line 3 inches (7.6 cm) from the bottom of the box and cut down the sides of the cardboard box to this height. Line the box with aluminum foil.
2. In a mixing bowl, mix the flour, salt, cooking oil, and 2 cups (500 ml) warm water together. Use your hands—it's a fun mess!
3. After you mix the ingredients thoroughly, add food coloring to make the dough brown or green. The amount you add depends on the color you want to get.
4. In the middle of the box, place the empty soda bottle and mold the dough around it to make a volcano shape. Build the mixture up high on the sides so that the bottle is covered up to the top (but so the opening is still visible). Let your volcano dry.
5. If you like, you can place tiny trees, houses, people, and animals made of dough on the sides of the volcano before it dries. Let it dry overnight.

6. Use the funnel to fill the bottle with 3 cups (750 ml) of warm water. Add 10 drops of red food coloring and the liquid dishwashing detergent. Remove the funnel and dry it completely.
7. Reinsert the funnel and pour the baking soda into the bottle.
8. Slowly add vinegar into the bottle. Sit back and watch your volcano erupt all over the place! The eruption begins immediately.

Go Fly a Kite!

In San Lucas Tolíman, children bring out kites for *Los Días de los Muertos*. This is the traditional beginning of the kite-flying season in the highlands around Guatemala's Lake Atitlán. Here's an activity in which you can make your own kite.

Materials

Adult assistance suggested
2 lightweight sticks, 30 and 36 inches (76 and
    91 cm) long (Balsa wood works well)
Knife
Glue
String
Scissors
Tissue paper
Markers
Tape
Ruler
Ribbon

1. With a knife, cut a narrow notch in each end of the sticks. This notch should be about ¼ inch (.5 cm) deep.

2. Using glue, attach the two sticks as shown in the diagram.

3. Thread the string through each notch to form a frame. After doing this, tie a knot in the end of the string to hold it in place. You should now have a frame that forms four sides of the kite.

4. Use markers to decorate a large piece of tissue paper that is big enough to cover the frame. You might want to draw an iguana or a quetzal bird with a long tail.

5. Lay the stick frame on the tissue paper. Fold paper over string and tape in place. Don't use too much tape—you want the kite to be as lightweight as possible.

6. Cut a *bridle* string that is about 4 feet (1.2 m) long. The bridle provides a place to tie your flying line, so that the flying line does not have to connect directly to the kite's body. Tie one end of the bridle string above the crosspiece and the other below it, as shown in diagram. Tie flying line to bridle.

7. Tie ribbon tail to kite. Find a wind and fly!

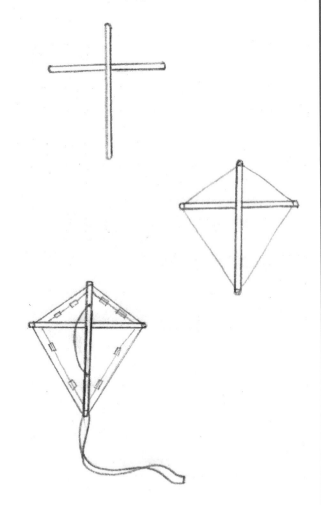

Two boys on the Atlantic Coast in Honduras gather cans from the beach to recycle. *Courtesy of Nancy Black and Mary C. Turck*

On the Atlantic Coast

This chapter moves from the mountainous highlands to the very different coastal lowlands. As geography changes, so do the lives of the people. This chapter introduces African immigrants who have brought their cultural contributions, the distinct Indian nations living along the coasts, and the descendants of British pirates who settled there.

Atlantic coastal areas of Central American countries differ dramatically from their interiors. English-speaking Belize, the smallest country in Central America, boasts coral reefs and miles of beaches. Panama, with the canal connecting the Atlantic and Pacific, also connects Central and South America. The Atlantic Coast is also called the *Caribbean Coast*. The Caribbean Sea is part of the Atlantic Ocean.

Coastal people are very different from those of the interior. In Nicaragua, Sumo and Miskito Indians and English-speaking descendants of pirates, colonists, and African slaves live along the coast. Honduran Garifunas struggle to maintain their distinct Afro-Caribbean culture. The San Blas Islands near Panama also preserve distinctive cultures.

Belize

On the eastern coast of Central America, the Atlantic Ocean crashes against the shore. Tiny, jewellike Belize perches between

Mexico and Guatemala. With only 250,000 people, Belize is the smallest country in Central America. The longest barrier reef in the Western Hemisphere stretches along its coast. Islands and coral reefs abound. Brilliant tropical fish below the water contrast with brightly plumed rainforest birds. Their jungle habitat steams under a tropical sun.

In Belmopan and along the coast, languages and people mix easily. English is the official language. Most Belizeans also speak a Creole dialect. Their ancestors were African slaves.

A smaller group of Afro-Indian Garifuna people arrived in 1802. They brought their own language with them. The Maya came after they fled Mexico in the nineteenth century, bringing their languages. *Mestizo* (mess-TEE-zoh) immigrants from Mexico brought Spanish at about the same time. *Mestizo* means "mixed" and refers to people whose ancestors include both Indians and Europeans. Chinese, Dutch-German Mennonites, East Indians, Lebanese, and

even descendants of British pirates mingle in a rich cultural stew.

Agriculture, tourism, and fishing are big business in Belize. Tourists enjoy scuba diving in the coral reefs, sunning on the beaches, and visiting Maya sites.

Garifuna

In 1635 two Spanish ships anchored off the shore of West Africa. Their captains bargained for human cargo. Soon the ships were packed full of captives, who lay in misery and chains below the decks. The two ships set sail for the Americas, eager to make a huge profit by selling slaves. They had made the trip before, as had other Spanish, Dutch, and English slave traders. This time, though, something went wrong for the slave traders. The ships were wrecked near the Caribbean island of St. Vincent.

The Africans escaped! Avoiding recapture, they settled on St. Vincent. There, they

Spik Kriol

In Belize, Creole, or Kriol, is a language made by combining English and African languages. There are varying pronunciations for these words, but here is one version and a few words in Kriol:

abak (ah-bahk): some time ago
agen (ah-gen): again, another time
chinchi (chin-chee): a tiny amount
da (dah): is, am, are; also at, on, in
deh (dey): am, is, are located
ih (ee): he, she, it
mi (mee): me
opstayz hous (ahp-stayz house): traditional Creole house, built high off the ground on posts. This keeps people away from snakes, high water, and insects at night—and provides a shady area for daytime activities.
uman (oo-mahn): woman
vex (veks): angry

Here are a few phrases in Kriol:

Ih da de teacha.	He/she is the teacher.
Ah no love ihn agen.	I don't love him any more.
Ihn deh pahn di boat.	He/she is on the boat.
Ih deh da skool.	He/she is at school.
Ih gaan luk fi dat.	He/she went to look for that.

Frying Plaintains

Belize borrows recipes from all of the many people who have made it home. As in other countries of the region, rice and beans are basic foods. They may be eaten with fish, chicken, pork, or beef—or with more exotic meats such as armadillo and *paca* (a nocturnal rodent)! Fried plantains are as popular in Belize as in other countries in the region, where they are called *tostones* (tos-TOH-nays).

Materials

Adult assistance suggested
6 plantains (available in larger grocery stores, or in Latin American groceries)
Sharp knife
Heavy frying pan
Cooking oil
Metal spatula or fork
Wax paper or paper bag
Rolling pin or rubber hammer
Paper towels
Salt

1. Plantains look like large bananas, but their skins are thicker and tougher. Before you begin, wash the plantains thoroughly.
2. The easiest way to prepare the plantains for cooking is to slice them diagonally. Each slice should be about 1-inch (2.5 cm) thick. Then, using your sharp knife, peel each slice.
3. When you have sliced the plantains, pour enough cooking oil into the pan to coat the bottom with a ⅓-inch (1 c) layer of oil and heat it.
4. When the oil is hot, gently slip the plantain slices into it. Use a metal spatula or a fork to do this to avoid burning your fingers.
5. Turn the plantain slices during cooking. When each side is a light, golden color, remove them carefully from the oil using the spatula. Place them on a flat surface and put wax paper or a paper bag over the slices. Pound them gently to flatten them, using the rolling pin or rubber hammer.
6. Return them to the frying pan and fry until golden brown on both sides.
7. Carefully remove slices from hot oil when they are done, using a spatula or fork. Place them on several layers of paper towel.
8. Salt them immediately to taste and let the oil drain off of the slices for a few minutes.

Eat while hot—they are delicious!

6 servings

married into the Carib Indian people. Indian and African cultures met and mixed. The new arrivals adopted Indian hunting and fishing practices. They preserved many of their African religious and musical traditions. Indian and African languages mingled. The new people called themselves the *Garifuna*.

At the end of the century, the British expelled the Garifuna from St. Vincent. They forcibly removed all of the Garifuna to Central America. Once again, the Garifuna people adapted to a new land. Today, a few thousand Garifuna live in Belize, and more live in Honduras, Nicaragua, Guatemala, Mexico, and on Caribbean islands.

Garifuna join the other Atlantic Coast residents of Honduras in building the nation's tourism industry. Coastal residents also work in the giant banana plantations. In Honduras, bananas grow in the Atlantic coastal lowlands.

Some Garifuna still grow *manioc*, an edible root plant, and *yucca*. Women grate, pound, wash, and cook the root crops, much as their ancestors did. Garifuna musicians play *punta* music, with rhythms that are claimed today as the Honduran national music. Conch shells, drums, turtle shells, and maracas come to life in the hands of skillful musicians.

Miskito Coast in Nicaragua

Thick jungles cover most of eastern Nicaragua. Deer, monkeys, and tapirs live in the tropical rainforest among orchids, trees, and exotic plants. Sandy beaches reach down to the Atlantic Ocean. Coral reefs surround the Corn Islands, about 50 miles (110 km) off the coast.

The Miskito people give their name to Nicaragua's Atlantic Coast. Some Miskitos live in Honduras, but most live in Nicaragua. Much smaller groups of Sumo and Rama Indians also live along the Miskito Coast, as do Garifuna people.

For centuries, Nicaraguan governments ignored the Atlantic Coast. No roads connected the capital city and the coast. No government officials visited there. The coastal people welcomed this "neglect." They

Making Music with Drums, Maracas, Güiros, and Claves

Drums carry the base line of Garifuna music. Two or three drums play in harmony. The *primera* (first) (pree-MEHR-ah), or heart, drum lays down the beat. The *segunda* (second) (say-GUN-da), or shadow, drum plays a complementary melody. A *tercera* (third) (tehr-SEHR-ah) drum joins with a bass line.

Drums may be made of wood, hollowed out and covered with tightly stretched animal skins. Sometimes one or two wires or strings are stretched over the drumhead. This produces an unusual buzzing sound when the drums are played.

Other percussion instruments join in. Maracas may originally have been made of gourds, but other materials will work. *Güiros* (WEE-rose) can be carved from wood, with different sized ridges producing different sounds.

Claves might be the simplest percussion instrument—just hit two sticks together in time to the music! Of course, you may want to paint your claves or decorate them with streamers or ribbons attached to the end that you hold.

Drums

Materials

Adult assistance suggested

Empty cans of various sizes, with and without lids (coffee cans or oatmeal containers work best)

Acrylic paint

Paintbrushes

Paper

Glue

Pieces of inner tube or other rubber

Pen

Ruler

Scissors

Rubber bands

Plastic lids fitting cans

Wooden chopsticks or dowels

1. Begin by decorating your empty cans and containers, which will be your drum containers. Paint or draw a design directly on the container or on paper that you then glue around the sides of the container. Choose a Central American design. (See page 41 for examples.) Wait until completely dry before continuing.

2. Next, you need to cover the open end of the drum container. If you have pieces of an old inner tube, begin by tracing a circle on them, using the bottom of the container you will use as the pattern.

3. Trace another circle around the outside of the first one that is two inches (five cm) larger than the container circle.

4. Cut out the larger circle.

5. Spread glue around the outside edges of the top (open end) of the container. Stretch the rubber tightly over the top of the container, pulling it down on the sides. Use rubber bands, in addition to the glue, to secure in place.

6. As an alternative to the rubber, you can use the plastic lids of the containers to cover them. Experiment by making a set of drums with different materials as drumheads. Each option will create a different drum sound. Use the bottom of a can as a metal drum head.

7. Try different kinds of drumsticks, such as wooden chopsticks or dowels, for different sound qualities. You can vary the sound of the drumsticks by wrapping the end that hits the drum with fabric or rubber bands.

Maracas

Materials

Adult assistance suggested

Empty soup or juice can

2 to 4 teaspoons (10 to 20 ml) uncooked rice
or beans

Glue

Pieces of inner tube or other rubber

Pen

Ruler

Scissors

Rubber bands

Plastic lids fitting cans

1. Place beans or rice in a clean and dry soup or
   juice can.
2. Cover the open end with rubber and glue or a
   plastic lid. (See steps 2–6 of the drum instructions on page 50.) Shake it up for music!
   Again, try different sizes and materials to produce different sounds.

Güiros

Traditional *güiros* are carved from dried, hollowed
gourds. Ridges carved into the gourd's surface are
scraped in a rhythmic pattern by a stick.

Materials

Adult assistance suggested

Dowels, 10 to 18 inches (25 to 46 cm) in
length, varying widths

Wooden chopsticks

Sandpaper

Carving knife or wood-working file

1. Sand the ends of the dowels smooth. If the
   chopsticks are splintery, sand them also.
2. Carve grooves into the dowel with a knife or
   wood-working file. The grooves should be fairly
   close together—about ¼-inch (.6 cm) apart will
   work well. Carve at least 10 grooves. Different
   sizes and depths of grooves produce different
   tones.
3. Use the chopstick to scrape across the grooves
   to make music. Vary speed, rhythm, and force
   to create different tones.

Claves

Claves are two highly polished and smooth sticks
of wood that measure 8 inches (20 cm) long and 1
inch (2.5 cm) in diameter. They are made from a
hardwood, preferably rosewood (available at craft
supply stores).

You can practice different musical rhythms
with claves. For example, you might pound in a
rhythm of "One, two. One, two, three." Or you
might use words to help set and maintain your
rhythm. Try pounding: "How are you?" and then
responding, "I'm fine."

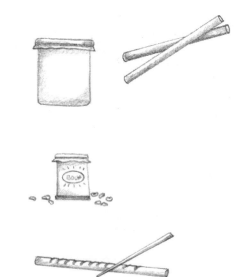

wanted no part of the central government. Sometimes the central government tried to send governors, impose laws, or collect taxes. The people of the Atlantic Coast fought back, sometimes with armed rebellion. During the 1980s, a compromise was reached. The Atlantic Coast was divided into two "autonomous" regions. (*Autonomous* means "self-governing," but the regions are in fact still part of the country of Nicaragua.) The Northern Autonomous Region includes most Miskito, Sumo, and Rama people.

From lobsters to gold to mahogany, the Atlantic Coast is rich in resources. Most of the resources are taken by outsiders, because the government has sold such contracts. Trees are cut by outside timber companies and sold at a good profit. Mining companies sell the gold. The people of the Atlantic Coast do not receive the benefits of the sale of these natural resources. They live in deep poverty. Many communities can be reached only by boat.

Bluefields is the largest town in the Northern Autonomous Region. Walking down the street in Bluefields, you might hear Miskito, Creole, English, or Spanish.

Four or five hundred years ago, English and Dutch pirates settled Bluefields. From its port, they swooped down to capture ships. British law arrived to officially colonize Bluefields in 1678. The descendants of pirates still live here, side by side with Garifuna and Miskito and mestizo people.

Afro-Caribbean culture and English flow down the Atlantic Coast through Costa Rica. Although the countries of Central America were colonized by the Spanish, the British held Caribbean islands. The Atlantic Coast is where the Caribbean and Central American cultures meet.

Panama

Panama both connects and divides the Americas. The Panama Canal, built a century ago, connects the Atlantic and Pacific oceans. Panama also lies between the Central American countries and the South American continent.

Until 1903 Panama was part of Colombia. The United States wanted to build a canal in Central America. At that time most trade was by ship. Ships had to travel all the way to the southern tip of South America and back up to cross from the Atlantic to Pacific oceans. A canal would make the trip much shorter and easier.

Colombia would not agree to U.S. terms for building a canal. Then Panama *seceded* (broke away) from Colombia. The United States encouraged Panama to rebel. The new country of Panama agreed immediately to let the United States build a canal.

Panama and the United States signed a treaty. The treaty gave the United States full control of the canal and the land for five miles (eight km) on each side. The canal took 10 years to build. It opened in 1914. A complex system of locks conducts ships safely through the canal. The canal shortcut saved a ship going from New York to San Francisco more than 7,000 miles (11,200 km).

The United States operated the Panama Canal, and U.S. soldiers guarded it. The United States ruled the canal zone. The people of Panama grew more and more unhappy with this arrangement. Finally, the two countries reached a new agreement. Panama

The Panama Canal. *Courtesy of Scott Bennan*

took back complete control of the canal in 1999.

Children in all the countries of the Americas share the common experience of going to school. In the next chapter, you will visit some of these schools.

Making a *Mola*

Most Kuna (also spelled Cuna) people live on the San Blas Islands. The San Blas Islands lie off the northern coast of Panama. Some Kuna live on the mainland, in the rainforest.

Kuna women sew intricate designs called *molas*. They are made from layers of colorful fabric. The designs are made by reverse appliqué. First, the artist sews together several layers of cloth. Each layer is a different color. Then, she cuts out a design, making the design smaller on each layer. She stitches down each layer. In the finished *mola*, all the colors show through.

Traditional *molas* show flowers, animals, fish, birds, and geometric designs.

Materials

Tracing paper
Pencil
Stiff paper
Scissors
Construction paper or felt of
    several colors
Glue

1. Begin by creating your design on tracing paper. You might choose a traditional design, such as a bird or fish. Or you might create a non-traditional design. In recent years, some Kuna women have agreed to make Santa Claus designs, because that's what foreign customers want to buy!

2. After you have sketched a design and are satisfied with it, trace it onto the stiff paper to make a template. (A *template* is the pattern you use for work.) You might want to include more than one design in your *mola*. Experiment with arrangements of the templates to be sure that you will like the look of the finished product.

3. Cut out the template.

4. Place the template on the construction paper that will be the top layer. Trace around it.

5. Cut the design out.

6. Set aside the template and the figure you have cut out. Keep the outside shape—the part that you would usually throw away. This is called the *negative template*.

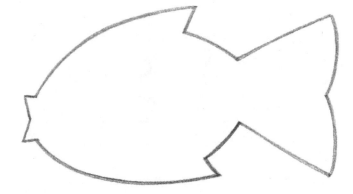

7. Place the negative template over the next color of paper or felt. Trace inside it, leaving about one-third of an inch (almost one cm) of room to make a slightly smaller design.

8. Cut out this second design. Again, set aside the shape and keep the negative template.

9. Repeat with each layer of paper or felt. You will end up with three or more negative templates, each slightly smaller than the next.

10. Carefully arrange these layers so that all the colors show. The smallest negative template will be on the bottom. The largest—the first one you cut out—will be on the top. Glue the layers together.

11. Cut small strips of the colored paper or felt. Decorate the background with a geometric arrangement of these small strips.

You have finished your *mola*! Frame it and keep it, or give it as a gift.

If you want to make a *mola* out of fabric, follow the same steps. With each shape, turn under and hand-stitch a tiny hem. Then sew the layers together, using very small stitches.

Girls play basketball at recess at their school in Guatemala. Some of the girls are wearing *traje*, the traditional Guatemalan clothing, and all the students are wearing sweaters, a main part of the school uniform. *Courtesy of Nancy Black and Mary C. Turck*

Going to School

This chapter looks at schools in Honduras, Mexico, and Guatemala. Each school is unique. Children of wealthy families go to private schools. Some go to boarding schools. Some go to the United States or Europe for a year in high school. In contrast, many poorer children can go to school only through sixth grade.

Yini Carolina's school

Yini Carolina Caballeros walks slowly down the dusty road. She is tired from a three-mile (five-km) trek under the blazing July sun. She has already worked in the family cornfield for hours.

Yini's school sits at the edge of the town of La Libertad in Honduras. Concrete blocks form its walls. The roof is made of tin. An outhouse stands nearby. There is no indoor plumbing. Water comes from a well.

Inside the school, a single teacher stands at the blackboard. About 30 students sit at desks crowded into the only room. A few posters hang on the walls. The students have made posters about planting trees. They have learned about the importance of trees to the environment.

Yini Carolina is 13 years old and in the fifth grade. Like other rural children, she often has to miss school to work in the fields. It may take her more than one year to complete a grade level.

Yini Carolina gets up at five o'clock every morning. Her mother lights a candle or gas lamp. Together they grind corn with a hand mill and make coffee and tortillas. Her six-year-old sister, Raquel Ortega, and her eight-year-old brother, Carlo Roberto Ortega, leave for school at about seven o'clock in the morning. They walk for an hour to get to school.

Like many Honduran schools, this one has two shifts. Older children, like Yini, go to school in the afternoon. More than 30 students crowd into the single room for each session.

If Yini Carolina wants to study beyond the sixth grade, she will have to leave her family. There is no other school in La Libertad. She would need to move to a bigger city, and her family would have to pay school fees. They would also have to pay for food, housing, and transportation.

Recess!

School children play some of the same games around the world. In the United States, kids play hopscotch. Using chalk, kids draw lines on sidewalks. They throw a stone and hop to the square, pick up the stone, and hop back again.

In Guatemala, the same game is called *Avión* (ah-vee-OHN). *Avión* means "airplane." The hopping girl holds her arms out for balance. She does look a little like an airplane. Where there are no sidewalks, students use sticks to draw lines in the dirt.

In Honduras, girls play the same game, only there it is called *La Rayuela*. Instead of numbers, they write the days of the week in the squares. Then they hop from day to day.

Girls also jump rope. Here is a Honduran rope-jumping chant:

Arroz con leche.	Rice with milk.
Me quiero casar	I want to marry
Con un muchacho	a boy
Quién sabe bailar	Who knows how
	to dance.
Contigo, sí.	Yes to you.
Contigo, no.	No to you.
Contigo, mi vida	With you, my love,
Me casaré yo!	I will get married!
Casate conmigo	Marry me
Que yo te daré	And I will give you

Zapatos y medias	Shoes and stockings
Color de café.	The color of coffee.

Soccer and kickball are favorites in Mexico and Central America. When there is no soccer ball, another ball will do. When there is no ball, children kick an old tin can or even a stone. No soccer field? Just make up some rules and play wherever you can.

La Vibora is a Mexican game. Students form a line. Each person puts his or her hands on the shoulders of the person in front. The line looks like a *vibora*, or sea serpent.

Two students make a bridge with their hands and hold them in an arch up in the air. The others march under the bridge. They sing: "*La vibora, vibora del mar, todos quieren a pasar*" ("The serpent, the serpent of the sea, everyone wants to pass").

On the last word of the song, the bridge children bring their hands down. Anyone captured is out of the game! The game can continue as long as you like or until everyone is out of the game. (In the United States, a very similar game is called "London Bridge.")

Capirucho

Do you know the game that uses a ball attached by a string to a cup or cone? You hold the cup, toss the ball, and try to catch it again. In Costa Rica, it's called *boliche* (bo-LEE-chay). In Mexico, it's *balero* (bah-LEHR-oh). In El Salvador, it's called *capirucho*. (kah-pee-ROO-choh). In Nicaragua, it's called *bola* (BOH-lah). Anywhere you play, *capirucho* is great fun!

Materials

Adult assistance suggested (if using a drill)
Cord or string (*la cuerda*—the cord), 10 to 18 inches (25 to 46 cm) long
Stick (*el palo*), about six inches (15 cm) long and ½-inch (1 cm) thick
Wooden or plastic cup
Wooden (or hard plastic) ball or cylinder, at least 1 inch (2.5 cm) in diameter, but small enough to fit in the cup
Drill (optional)

1. Wrap one end of the cord securely around the middle of the stick. Tie it in place. Then glue or tape the cup securely to the top half of the stick.
2. Tie the other end of the cord through the cylinder or ball. If you are using a ball, you will have to drill a hole through the center so that you can attach the cord.
3. To play, you swing the string to try to catch the cylinder or the ball in the cup. See how many times in a row you can do it.
4. Beginners play three strikes and you're out. After three tries, it's the next person's turn. More skillful players get just one try.

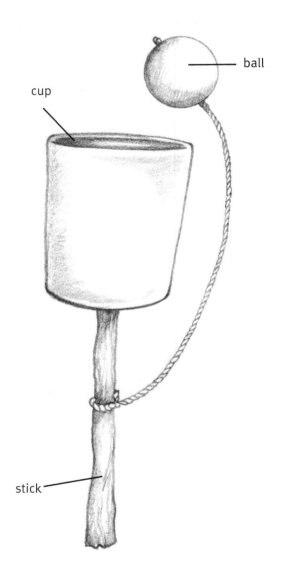

ball

cup

stick

School Schedules

Throughout Central America, the school year runs from February to November. Like Yini's school, many others have a split day. In that way, one school can teach twice as many children.

The first six years of school are called *primaria* (pree-MAH-ree-ah). Even small towns may have primary schools. Children often walk long distances to get to school. Most parents want their children to get an education. They try hard to keep their children in school for the first six years.

Many students, like Yini, attend school only through sixth grade. Some drop out even earlier. They may be needed to work at home. Their parents may lack money to buy pencils and paper.

In cities, too, most young children walk to school. Wealthy children go to private schools. Their parents can afford to pay high tuition and fees. They may take city buses to school. If their families have enough money, someone may drive them to school.

Even some poor children go to private schools. Private schools are run by churches. Church-run schools are not as fancy as rich private schools, but they have better facilities than public schools.

After *primaria*, the next three years are called *plan basico* (plahn BAH-see-coh). This is like junior high school. Students often need to live away from home to go to *basico*. A few years ago, Guatemala had 11,349 *primarias* and only 1,793 *basicos*.

Education costs rise as students get older. Junior high schools require books and uniforms. Often they charge tuition. Only larger towns or cities have *basico* schools.

Even fewer cities have high schools, which are called *colegios* (coh-LAY-hee-ohs). *Colegio* prepares students for college or vocational (trade) training. Few students go beyond nine years of school. For most people, the costs are just too high.

In Guatemala in 1996, only 39 percent of all adults had more than three years of schooling; more than one in three had no schooling at all.

Yarn Painting

Art projects are always favorite activities in schools. The Huichol Indians make beautiful yarn paintings. You—or your class in school—can make these paintings, too.

Materials

Cardboard or poster board
Pencil
Yarn, black and bright colors
Scissors
Glue

1. Draw a simple picture on the cardboard or poster board. Here are a few examples to give you an idea:
2. Cut a piece of black yarn that is long enough to cover the outline of the entire drawing.
3. Squeeze a thin line of glue on top of a small part of the outline. Start with one end of the black yarn and attach it to the paper, placing it on top of the glue. Push down to adhere.
4. Continue until you have covered the entire outline of your drawing in black yarn. You may also choose to cover the inside lines of the design with black yarn.
5. Choose colors for the smaller inner sections of the design such as the wings of the bird, the bottom half of the fish, and so forth. Beginning at the edge of each design, just inside the black outline, glue the yarn around in a never-ending circle until you reach the center of the section.
6. Finally, fill in the background. Again, begin at the outer edge and make smaller and smaller circles.

A City School in Comayagua

Comayagua is a city of about fifty thousand in Honduras. Students from middle or even upper-class families study at the Instituto Imaculada in Comayagua. The Instituto is like a high school. It is a private school, run by the Catholic Church. The nine hundred students at the Instituto have completed six years of *primaria* and three years of *basico*.

Some students come from Comayagua. Many others come from distant towns. In addition to paying tuition, these students must find a place to live and pay room and board. Some teenage girls stay with two Catholic nuns at a convent. Most of their families pay for their room and board. Some families cannot afford to pay. The nuns beg for money from individuals and charities so that these girls may continue to attend school. The nuns do not want the poor girls to feel different from the richer girls, so they make all the girls at the convent sew their own dresses. That way, they all are dressed alike.

The girls rise at 5 A.M.; breakfast is ready at 5:30 and consists of oatmeal, beans, and tortillas. They leave for school by 6:20, having said a morning prayer and cleaned the house, putting away belongings and mopping the floors. The school is only a 15- or 20-minute walk away from the convent. One of the Catholic nuns works at the school, and the other works in another program.

The girls return from school at about 1 P.M. and eat their midday meal. They have free time until 3 P.M., and then from 3 to 5 P.M. they study. Then, it's time for supper, and later for cleaning up the house again. A second study time lasts from 7 to 8 P.M. Then, the girls are free until bedtime at 9 P.M.

If students want to go on to college, they must complete a two-year course of study. To get a computer degree, they study three years. Many of the girls living at the convent want to become bilingual secretaries. That is also a three-year program.

Families make sacrifices so that their children can attend school. They pay for lodging in the city. They pay for food, uniforms, books, and tuition.

Visiting a School in Guatemala

Lemoa is a small town in Guatemala. Its single school is a *primaria*. Many of the children in Lemoa grow up speaking Quiché (kee-CHAY), a Maya language. When they begin school, they first spend a year learning Spanish. Their teachers usually speak only Spanish.

About 140 students attend the elementary school in Lemoa. A first-grade classroom is tiny and crowded with desks. The youngest children study only language and mathematics.

The third-grade classroom is larger. Third-grade students range from 7 to 13 years of age. Many work in the fields and come to school late or not at all. Señora Eugenia, their teacher, has taught here for 17 years. She taught the parents of some of her current students.

Education and Politics

Students throughout Mexico and Central America often become involved in politics. They may see that only a tiny number of young people get to go to high school or college. They may see large differences between rich and poor people. If adults strike or demonstrate, students often join them. Sometimes students lead political protests.

Teachers in Central America are paid very little. In Honduras in 2002, elementary-school teachers earned about $1.38 per hour. Teachers in some Honduran cities went on strike because they did not receive paychecks at all. The government simply did not send the checks.

In Guatemala, teachers went on strike in 2003. They demanded more money for salaries and schools. The Guatemalan teachers eventually won a pay raise to a beginning salary of $190 per month, with a top salary of about $360 per month.

According to government statistics, the average family of five in Guatemala needed $308 per month just to live above the poverty level in 1998. The cost of basic food needs alone was $169. As you can see, the basic teacher's salary barely buys food for the family, while even the highest teacher's salary is not much more than poverty level.

When teachers go out on strike, students often join them.

64

La Huelga (The Strike), A Stage Play

A *union* is an organization of workers who join together to try to get better pay and working conditions. When workers *strike*, they stop working until the employer meets their demands or until both sides agree to a contract for a higher hourly wage, improved working conditions, or better work hours. During the strike, union members may form a picket line. *Picketing* means that people march, usually with signs that reflect the grievances of the workers. Workers may picket the employer, the place of work, or even government offices.

This play illustrates the issues that lead teachers and students out of the classroom and onto the picket line.

Characters

Señorita Estrella, a teacher (teachers always dress formally, so she must wear a dress or skirt and blouse)

Diego, a student (students usually wear uniforms, and male students wear dark pants and a white shirt)

Daniela, Diego's cousin (female students wear a dark skirt and a white shirt)

Señora Ramirez, Diego's mother

Señor Ramirez, Diego's father

Abuelo, Diego's grandpa

Extras: If there are more people who want to be in the play, extra parts include Diego's three brothers at the dinner table, other students in the school, and marchers on the picket line.

Props

Map

Pointer

Books

Desks

Pencils

Paper

Table and chairs

Bright tablecloth

Plates

Cups

Signs

Markers

Scene 1: At School

There is a map at the front of the room. There are two (or more) desks for students. The teacher has a pointer. Students have one book, pencil, and paper at each desk.

As the play begins, three characters are in a schoolroom. They introduce themselves. If there are extras, they sit quietly at the other desks, writing or reading. When the teacher speaks, everyone stops what he or she is doing to pay attention to her.

Señorita Estrella: (comes to center front and bows to audience) My name is Marta Estrella. I teach school in Comayagua. I teach in a *basico*, which is similar to a junior high school in the United States. I am 25 years old. I have been teaching for three years. I live with my uncle and aunt. I wish I could live on my own, but I don't make nearly enough money.
(She walks to blackboard or map, picks up pointer, and stands, pointing at map.)

Diego: (comes to center front and bows to audience) My name is Diego Ramirez. I am 13 years old. I live in Comayagua with my parents, my grandfather, my three brothers, and my cousin, Daniela. I am in the first year of *basico*. I want to become an architect. I study very hard. Architects need to do well in school. (Diego goes to desk, sits down, and begins writing.)

Daniela: (comes to center front and bows to audience) My name is Daniela Ramirez. I am 13 years old. I live in Comayagua with my aunt and uncle, my grandfather, and my cousins. I am in my first year of *basico*. I want to become a teacher. My parents and brothers and sisters live in La Libertad. There is no *basico* school in La Libertad. I live with my aunt and uncle here so that I can go to school. (Daniela goes to desk, sits down, and begins writing.)

Señorita Estrella: (addressing the class) Attention, please. I have an important announcement. Tomorrow there will be no school. (Students cheer.)

Señorita Estrella: Attention, *please*! The reason there will be no school is that there will be a strike. The teachers are going on strike.

Diego: (raising his hand, waits until teacher calls on him to speak) Señorita Estrella, why is there a strike?

Señorita Estrella: We are going on strike to demand more money for schools.

Daniela: (raising her hand, waits until teacher calls on her to speak) I think we need more money for books. I want to study English, but the book is missing too many pages.

Diego: (raising his hand, waits until teacher calls on him to speak) I agree. We also need a real soccer field.

Señorita Estrella: Books and a soccer field would be nice. But before those, schools need teachers. And we need to live. We have not been paid for six weeks. We cannot work without being paid.

Daniela: (raising her hand, waits until teacher calls on her to speak) Who pays the teachers?

Diego: (raising his hand, waits until teacher calls on him to speak) I know—the government pays teachers. But why didn't the government pay you?

Señorita Estrella: You know that our country is poor. We do not have a lot of money. And the government uses the money for many things. But they always have money for armies. Schools are important. They need to pay teachers, too.

Daniela: (raising her hand, waits until teacher calls on her to speak) Can we help you? Can we go on strike, too?

Diego: (raising his hand, waits until teacher calls on him to speak) Yes—it's our school, too. And you deserve to be paid for your work. It is a matter of justice!

Señorita Estrella: I don't know. I don't know what your parents would say. But tomorrow morning we will be making signs. Then we will start to march at 1 P.M.

Scene II: At the Dinner Table in Daniela and Diego's Home

The dinner table is a little crowded. All the family members sit there, as close together as needed to fit around the table. The table may be covered with a brightly colored tablecloth. It should have a plate and cup or glass for each person.

Señora Ramirez: What happened in school today, Diego?

Diego: Not much. You know, the usual.

Daniela: Diego! That's not true! Remember the strike!

Diego: Oh, yes—I almost forgot. *Mama*, *Papá*, there is a strike tomorrow.

Abuelo: You can't strike. You don't work. Strikes are for workers. Workers strike to get better wages. They strike for justice.

Señor Ramirez: Besides, you need to study. You won't get into the *colegio* unless you study hard. And you need to go all the way through the *cole-gio* and to the university to become an architect.

Daniela: This is a teacher strike. They are striking for more money for schools. They haven't been paid.

Abuelo: Well, then, they should strike! Teachers are workers, too.

Señora Ramirez: So, there will be no school because the teachers are striking?

Daniela: Yes, and we want to strike, too. We want to support them.

Diego: That's right. Teachers need to be paid. And the government should give more money to schools.

Abuelo: If the children go, they will learn more than they do in school.

Señora Ramirez: Wait a minute, wait a minute. Strikes are for adults. Children do not strike. The police come when there are strikes. People get hurt.

Señor Ramirez: I understand that you want to help your teachers. But *Mama* is right. Picket lines are no place for children.

Daniela: But I don't want the police to hurt Señorita Estrella! If we go, we can protect her.

Diego: I don't know. If there are going to be police, there could be violence. I don't want to get shot.

Abuelo: I would go if I could. But I have a job, too. If I don't go to my job, I get fired.

Señor Ramirez: Me, too. You know how hard it is to get a job these days. I can't just take a day off to go and march.

Daniela: But we can. We can't go to school if the teachers are on strike. We can march with them. Students can strike, too.

Diego: We could go in the morning. We could help the teachers make signs. We wouldn't have to march.

Señora Ramirez: Yes—you can help make the signs.

That seems safe enough. And the teachers are right—they deserve to be paid for their work. The government always has money for the army. They should instead use the money for our children's education.

Scene III: On the Picket Line

As the scene opens, Daniela and Diego are finishing the lettering on a sign at center stage front. Other people are already standing in a line at stage right, carrying their signs. The others include both students and teachers. The signs have various slogans such as "Huelga! Support Our Teachers"; "Pay Teachers, Not Politicians"; and "Money for Schools."

Daniela: I know it might be dangerous. But I am going to march anyway. This is the right thing to do.

Diego: But my father said picket lines are no place for children.

Daniela: I know, but he's not my father. Besides, he didn't actually say, "Diego, you can't go."

Diego: That's true. And Abuelo said he would go if he could. Abuelo thinks it is right to strike.

(Señorita Estrella approaches the cousins.)

Señorita Estrella: That's a very nice sign. Are you going to march to the government center with us?

Daniela: I am.

Diego: I know my father doesn't want us to go. But he didn't exactly say no.

Señorita Estrella: I know my mother doesn't want me to march, either. She wants me to be safe. She's afraid the police will attack, as they have before. But I need to stand up for what is right.

Daniela: I feel the same way. It is important to stand up for justice.

Diego: My father may be angry. But I think you are right. Besides, I don't want you two to get hurt. I will go with you.

(The three join the line of marchers, and they march across the stage and exit to the left.)

Questions for Further Discussion

1. If workers go on strike by stopping work, how do students go on strike?
2. Why did the students in the play want to go on strike?
3. What are some other reasons that students might have for going on strike?
4. How could other people support the striking teachers? How could they support other striking workers?
5. Could students form a union? What issues would a students' union organize around?

Unions in the United States

Workers began organizing unions in the United States more than a hundred years ago. They believed that workers needed to band together to get a better deal from richer, more powerful employers. Over the years, unions won safety laws, a minimum wage, the 40-hour workweek, and many other things workers take for granted today. The AFL–CIO (American Federation of Labor–Congress of Industrial Organizations) is a large federation of many United States unions.

Unions in Guatemala

Guatemala has laws to protect workers' rights to organize unions. Unfortunately, the government of Guatemala does not enforce those laws. Workers are often fired when they try to organize unions. Sometimes union organizers are threatened or even killed. Despite the danger, workers continue to organize to win better pay, working conditions, and respect for their rights. For more information on labor unions in Latin America, visit the U.S. Labor Education in the Americas Project at www.usleap.org.

Schools teach about history and language and how the society works. But culture includes more than education. The next chapter introduces readers to some of the art and poetry of Mexico and Central America.

Learn a Little Spanish!

escuela (ess-KWAY-lah): school

maestra (my-ESS-trah): female teacher

maestro (my-ESS-troe): male teacher

estudiante (ess-too-dee-AHN-tay): student

pupitre (poo-PEE-tray): desk

pluma (PLOO-mah): pen

lápiz (LAH-pees): pencil

papel (pah-PELL): paper

estudiar (ess-TOO-dee-ahr): to study

aprender (ah-pren-DARE): to learn

practicar (prahk-tee-CAHR): to practice

huelga (WELL-gah): strike

This mural on a wall in León, Nicaragua, was created by local artists to show their memory of the revolution. *Courtesty of Mary C. Turck*

6

Art and Poetry

Art and poetry express people's deepest feelings. But have you ever thought of art expressed in a giant puppet? Or of poetry written by a gun-toting revolutionary? These are just a few of the fascinating topics ahead.

And that warm, sweet, green odor of Central America.

The white houses with red-tiled roofs and with wide sunny eaves,

and a tropical courtyard with a fountain and a woman by the fountain.

And the heat making our beards grow longer.

What scenes return to my memory now!

(From "With Walker in Nicaragua" by Ernesto Cardenal, translated by Jonathan Cohen)

Ernesto Cardenal was a poet and a priest. He was also a revolutionary, and he became Cultural Minister of Nicaragua in 1979. A bitter political foe of Vice-President Cardenal criticized him sharply. He said that Cardenal had abandoned his calling as a poet for the less important work of politics! The critic was serious. In Nicaragua, poetry is important and highly honored work.

Art, poetry, and politics often go hand in hand. Poems speak of politics. Artists express their convictions.

In Mexico, Diego Rivera combined painting and politics. He wrote that if an artist "won't put down his magic brush and head the fight against the oppressor, then he isn't a great artist." He believed that art could—and should—change the world.

Rivera's painting celebrated the beauty of poor people. His grand murals in public places brought art to ordinary people.

Rubén Darío–Nicaraguan Genius

Rubén Darío began to write poetry in 1877. He was 10 years old. His first poem was published when he was 13. At 14 he left his native Nicaragua. Darío moved to El Salvador. It was the first of many moves. During his life, Darío traveled widely. At times, he lived in Chile, Argentina, Spain, and France. He also visited the United States and many European countries. During his life, Darío experienced both poverty and wealth.

Painting a Mural

Murals often tell stories. Diego Rivera painted frescoes in Mexico's National Palace. The frescoes show the history of Mexico. A mural by Rivera in Detroit, Michigan, shows autoworkers and the auto industry.

People paid Rivera to paint on walls of buildings. If you paint the wall of the school, you are more likely to get into big trouble! So where can you paint a mural? And what kind of story do you want to tell? Find a space you want to paint and ask for permission to do this. Then begin.

Materials

Pencils for sketching

Paper

Graph paper for planning

Ruler

Roll of newsprint, poster board, or other large surface

Tempera paints

Paintbrushes, various sizes

1. First, you need a big idea. Write down a few words explaining your idea. Here are a couple of suggestions:

   My family tree: Its roots reach down to a potato farmer in Ireland, a shoemaker in Germany, and great-grandparents driving a covered wagon across the prairie. Its branches reach upward. Tangled in the branches are images of myself and brothers and sisters and cousins. One boy paddles a canoe. Another plays baseball. A girl plays soccer. Another is almost buried under a stack of books.

   My school: This mural is divided into different rooms. One room is filled with frogs, snakes, and a science teacher. In the gym, students hang from ropes and run around a track and shoot baskets. Huge black quarter notes nearly break the walls of the music room.

   Dream up your own idea!

2. Decide how big your mural will be. Find a place to paint it. You might use newsprint or poster board. You might use an old refrigerator box.

3. Use graph paper to plan your mural. Measure the area of the surface you will paint. Using your graph paper, figure out the scale, based on the size of the surface you will be using. A single square on the graph paper might represent one square foot (0.1 sq m) or four square inches (25 sq cm).

   For example, you might plan to paint a mural on a hallway wall that is 11 feet (3.4 m) long and 8 feet (2.4 m) high. Your graph paper measures 9 inches (23 cm) wide and 12 inches (30 cm) tall. You can use 1 inch (2.5 cm) on the graph paper to represent 12 inches (30 cm) on the wall. Count the number of squares that make up one inch. If there are four squares per inch, then each square on the graph paper would be one-quarter of a foot, or 3 inches (7.6 cm) on the wall.

4. Decide which images go where. Sketch a rough design on the graph paper. Use a pencil and be prepared to erase and make changes.

5. Transfer your design to the wall (or poster board) where the mural will go. Use the graph paper as a guide. Draw light lines on the wall. Draw the first line from floor to ceiling at the left of your wall. Then, draw another line, parallel to the first and 1 foot (30 cm) from it. Continue until you have marked off 1-foot (30-cm) squares on the whole wall. Sketch in outlines from the graph paper onto the mural. You may want to include words as well as pictures.

6. Draw in details of each image.

7. Now you are ready to paint! Paint one color at a time. Let each color dry before you paint the next. Clean your brushes carefully between colors so the colors don't mix.

Display your mural for the world to see! Enjoy the compliments you receive.

Diego Rivera

Born in 1886, Diego Rivera was called the greatest Mexican painter of the 20th century. He studied fresco painting in Europe. (*Frescoes* are murals and paintings that are painted on fresh plaster.) Rivera liked to paint where many people could see his work. His frescoes covered entire walls. He painted Mexican history. He painted the struggles of workers. He painted in the United States. In 1933 Rivera was commissioned to paint a mural in Rockefeller Center in New York City. The Rockefellers were one of the wealthiest families in the United States. They wanted a mural that would show "Man at the Crossroads," with the social and scientific changes of the 20th century. In part of the mural, Rivera depicted a giant workers' demonstration, with the workers waving red banners and led by Vladimir Lenin, the Russian communist leader. The Rockefellers said that Lenin had to be removed. Rivera refused and, angered by the demands, destroyed the mural. Rivera painted in Mexico, too. He died in 1957.

As a journalist, Darío wrote for newspapers. As a diplomat, he served both Nicaragua and Colombia. As a writer, he expressed his own "interior melody." In poetry, he spoke of Latin America's heritage:

> " . . . the America of Moctezuma and Atahualpa,
> the aromatic America of Columbus,
> Catholic America, Spanish America,
> the America where noble Cuauthémoc said:
> "I am not in a bed of roses"—our America,
> trembling with hurricanes, trembling with Love:
> O men with Saxon eyes and barbarous souls,
> our America lives. And dreams. And loves.
> And it is the daughter of the Sun. Be careful."

> (From "To Roosevelt," in *Selected Poems of Rubén Darío.* Translated by Lysander Kemp. Austin: University of Texas, 1988.)

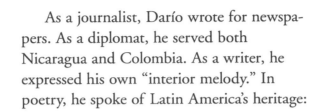

Darío said he thought in French and wrote in Spanish. His mixture of European and American tradition transformed Latin American poetry. He led the poetic movement called *modernism*.

Gioconda Belli: A Revolutionary Poet

Gioconda Belli's life story reads like a novel. She began as a child of wealth. She grew into a gun-toting revolutionary. Her life includes world travel, an earthquake, childbirth, a secret life as a revolutionary, and *exile* (forced absence from one's country of birth)—all before the age of 30. She is, said another writer, an "unfairly beautiful poet."

Belli's ancestors came to Nicaragua from Italy. Born in 1948, she grew up in a wealthy, aristocratic family. She attended schools in Spain and the United States. She wanted to become a doctor. Her parents said no. So Belli married at age 18 and soon had a baby.

Her husband wanted her to stay home with the baby. She insisted on working. Her husband was sad and quiet. She wanted life and joy. Their marriage had little chance of success. Belli kept on working and writing poetry. She soon fell in love with a man she called "the Poet."

Writing Poetry

Poets find inspiration in many different places. Sometimes they write about grand topics such as life, love, beauty, and justice. Sometimes they write about small topics such as a cat, a snowflake, or a smile. Sometimes they think hard about which word is just the right word. Sometimes the words just seem to flow like a river. Here are some opportunities for you to explore your own self-expression through poetry. Try three different ways of writing poetry.

Materials

Paper
Pencil or pen

The "I Like" Poem

1. Choose a person, place, or thing.
2. Write down a one-word name for your subject.
3. Write down things you like about that person, place, or thing. You can write in sentences or phrases. Put each reason on a new line. Here is an example:

Winter
long nights
soft snow
glowing lights
Christmas tree smell

4. Now add in your "I like" phrase to start off your poem. Adjust each phrase, if you care to, to more specifically describe a moment, place, or thing. For example:

Winter
I like winter because . . .
snow sparkles at night
Christmas lights glitter
we light candles
we have vacation.

The Free-Verse Poem

Free verse is poetry without rhymes. In writing free verse, you play with words, paint word pictures, explore sounds and images. Choose a topic. Here are some ideas for topics: someone you know, something you like, a pet, a place, and a time of day. Here is an example of free verse:

Nora
My cat
growls in the night
chases invisible monsters
meows for treats
purrs for petting.

1. Choose one of the topics listed above or think up your own topic that inspires you.
2. Put your pencil to the paper and record all the thoughts that come to mind when you think about your chosen topic, writing a poem like the above example.

The Acrostic Poem

An *acrostic* poem uses sets of letters (such as the initial or final letter of each line) to form a word or phrase related to the topic of the verse. In the following example look at the first letter of each line to find the word "justice."

1. Pick a topic.
2. Write the topic down on your paper, with the first letter on the first line, second letter on the second line, and so on, so that you are writing your topic word vertically.
3. Write down words or phrases related to your topic using the one letter on each line as inspiration. Each word or phrase must begin with the letter on that line. They must also relate to your topic, which might also be the title of the poem. This one's a bit more challenging.

Belli's life was in turmoil. So was her country. Nicaragua suffered under a brutal dictator, Anastasio Somoza. He stole money sent for earthquake victims. He tortured and killed political opponents. Nicaraguans lived in terrible poverty. Somoza and his associates controlled all the country's wealth.

Revolution was in the air. The Sandinistas planned to overthrow Somoza. They promised to end repression. They spoke of a country with education and health care for all. They said the country's wealth must be shared. Belli decided to join the revolution.

Her decision was not easy. She wrote later about a conversation with a friend: "I said, 'I have a daughter, I am afraid.' He said, 'Well you have to do it for your daughter because if you don't do it, your daughter is going to have to do it. If your parents had done it, you wouldn't have to be doing it.' It's true. That settled the question for me."

Revolution took her away from home. She went on secret missions, making trips to Cuba and to Europe. Then, she was forced into exile, since the Somoza government sought to capture her and put her in jail. In 1979 the revolution triumphed. The Sandinistas took over the government. Belli returned to Nicaragua. She was 31 years old.

Belli continued to work for the revolution. She also kept on writing, both about her personal life and about her experiences in working for revolution. Her books were translated into many languages.

Eventually, she married a U.S. citizen. Today, she and her husband divide their time between their home countries. For part of the year, they live in California. For the other part of the year, they live in Nicaragua.

Ordinary and Extraordinary Art

Folk art is the art of the people. It uses basic materials and is a craft form that is passed from generation to generation. It is often tied to religious and cultural events, and

The Tree of Life

In the Central Highlands of Mexico, folk artists create a design called the *Tree of Life*. The tree usually shows the biblical creation of life. Adam and Eve appear on the tree. So do bright birds and flowers and fruits. A snake twines among the branches.

Sometimes the Tree of Life is a sculpture to hang on the wall or stand on a table. Sometimes it is a candleholder. You can make a sculptured Tree of Life.

Materials

Adult assistance suggested
Pot
Measuring cups
Measuring spoons
1 cup (250 ml) salt
2 cups (500 ml) flour
4 teaspoons (20 ml) cream of tartar
2 cups (500 ml) cold water
Wooden spoon
Plastic wrap
Tracing paper
Pencil
Cardboard or foam core
Scissors or X-acto knife
Acrylic paints, green and bright colors
Paintbrushes
Glue

1. In a pot, mix together salt, flour, and cream of tartar. Add water and mix well with a wooden spoon. Cook on medium heat. Stir constantly until the dough looks like mashed potatoes. Remove from heat and cool. When clay is cool, cover in plastic wrap until ready to use.
2. Trace tree pattern onto cardboard or foam core. Cut out carefully.
3. Paint the tree green.
4. Break off small pieces of clay. Model them into the shapes of Adam and Eve, birds, flowers, fruits, and leaves. Set aside to dry for a day.
5. After clay figures have dried, paint them with bright colors. Let the paint dry.
6. Arrange the objects on the tree and glue them in place.

designs often depict religious celebrations or cultural figures. Folk art takes many forms.

In Oaxaca, Mexico, a man carves and paints long-tailed cats. In San Lucas Tolíman, Guatemala, a woman sits on the ground and weaves. Using her loom, she creates complex designs, with multicolored threads turning into flowers or birds. She learned this craft from her mother. She also creates new works of art. In Honduras, a boy carves wooden bowls. A woman sits next to a winding road. She weaves baskets and sells them to those passing by. Each of these people creates folk art.

Folk art exists in the United States, too. Quilts are an example of U.S. folk art. For centuries, women have stitched scraps of material into complex designs. Using old clothes and fabric left over from other sewing projects, they created colorful works of art. Then, these works of art were used to keep people warm on winter nights and were given to young couples beginning their lives together.

When the Spanish invaded Mexico, they brought their religion with them. Throughout Mexico and Central America, people already practiced Aztec and Maya religions. The Spanish conquerors believed these religions were evil. They wanted everyone to become Christian. They destroyed Maya and Aztec temples and books. They built Christian churches over Maya holy places. They ordered people to stop practicing old religions. They said everyone must be baptized. Everyone must become Christian.

Most Mexican and Central American people are still baptized. Most are Catholic. A growing minority are Evangelical (Protestant Christians). These religions are part of the heritage of conquest.

Over the centuries, indigenous religions survived. In Guatemala's highlands, Maya priests still perform religious ceremonies. They pray to Maya gods inside Christian churches that were built over old Maya holy places. They combine parts of traditional

Creating an *Ofrenda*

An *ofrenda* is like an altar. People make *ofrendas* in their homes. They decorate the *ofrenda* to remind themselves of someone special.

Sometimes an *ofrenda* honors God or a saint. (*Saints* are holy people who are dead. They are remembered for the good deeds they performed during their lifetimes.) Other *ofrendas* honor a family member or friend who has died. These are a kind of memorial for the dead.

Materials

Adult assistance suggested
Small wooden or plastic box, with a cover (such as a shoebox)
Pretty fabric or scarf
Scissors
Embroidery floss or ribbons (optional)
Needles (if using embroidery floss)
Thread (if using ribbons)
Memory objects (things that the person owned or enjoyed, such as marbles, collector's cards, or a favorite book)
Flowers
Heavy cardboard
Glue

Photos or pictures of the person you want to honor
Crepe paper
Votive candle in a glass container

1. Begin with the altar. The wooden or plastic box will be the base of the altar. If you are using a shoebox, place it upside down. Cut a piece of fabric large enough to completely cover the outside of the box with its lid. You may want to decorate the fabric with embroidery stitching or ribbons.
2. Arrange the flowers or memory objects on top of the altar.
3. Cover the cardboard with fabric, gluing in place. Then, arrange the photos on the cardboard and glue them in place. Stand the cardboard up behind the altar.
4. You may place another image in the center of the altar. The image might be a statue of a holy person. It might be a picture of a family member who has died.
5. Use crepe paper to make a frame around the image. Cut a long strip of crepe paper, about two inches (five cm) wide. Pleat one side of the paper, fanning out the other side. (*Pleating* means folding the paper in a series of parallel, but alternating folds, so that it looks like an accordion.)
6. Place the votive candle, in its container, on the altar. Be very careful to keep the candle inside a non-flammable container. Always get parents' permission before lighting the candle. Never leave a burning candle unattended.

Optional: After lighting the candle, sit quietly in front of the altar and think of the person who is framed in the middle of your altar. Think about why you have included the mementos you chose. If the photo is of a loved one, try to remember a time when you were with this person and an activity you shared. What do you feel? Remember this feeling. Now, whenever you revisit your altar, you can return to this special feeling about your loved one who is no longer here.

Maya religious practice with Christian rituals. Both Maya and Christian religious traditions find expression in folk art.

Las Gigantonas

In León, Nicaragua, people create *Gigantonas* each year. *Gigantonas* are giant puppets. Each one is at least 10 feet (3 m) tall. They are women with dark skin and hair. They look like beautiful *indigenous* (native) women.

For hundreds of years, light-skinned people dominated business and politics in Nicaragua. The *Gigantona* ritual makes fun of them. She represents the dark-skinned people of Latin America. When she appears, she is bigger than anyone else. She is the most powerful and most beautiful puppet, towering over everyone, showing great strength.

The *Gigantonas* dance through the streets of León. They perform in December and January. Musicians accompany them. The streets resound with the sound of snare drums. People sing songs they have composed. Often the songs make fun of government officials. Children also follow the *Gigantonas*. They make music with drums or plastic milk bottles.

Some *Gigantonas* have smaller friends. The friend is called *Pepe Cabezon*, or "Big-Head Pepe." Pepe runs or dances after the *Gigantona*. He is a comic character. The *Gigantona* is dignified. Pepe is foolish.

The next chapter turns from art and poetry to the nitty-gritty of cooking tortillas and planting corn. Featuring food and work, this chapter will introduce activities of daily life in Mexico and Central America.

Political Puppets

Begin by imagining a story you'd like to tell with puppets. Maybe your puppet heroine is a student leader at school. Perhaps she heads a movement for better school lunches. Can your puppet heroine accomplish this on her own? Who will need to help her? Whom does she need to talk with? Of course, you will want to make several puppets. Then they can play different roles in the story.

Materials

Soap bottles
Styrofoam balls, about 4 inches (10 cm) in
    diameter (from craft supply store)
Glue
Duct tape
Yardsticks
Fabric, brightly colored
Scissors
Buttons
Needle
Thread
Ribbons, braid, and trim
Cotton or polyester fiberfill

1. Use the soap bottle for the body. Glue a Styrofoam ball on top for the head.
2. Use duct tape to attach the stick to the back of the bottle. You will use the stick to make the puppet move and dance.
3. Cut a piece of fabric that will cover the head, and then cover the head with this fabric. Tie the fabric securely to the neck of the bottle using the ribbons.
4. Glue on eyes made of a different color of fabric or of buttons.
5. For the upper torso, wrap the top part of the bottle with one fabric. Be sure the ends of the fabric overlap. This will also cover the top-most part of the stick. Glue the fabric in place.
6. Using the same fabric cut two pieces that measure about 8 inches (20 cm) long and 3 inches (7.5 cm) wide. Fold the fabric so that the long edges are together and the wrong side of the fabric is on the outside.
7. For each arm, sew along the long side of the fabric, making a tube.
8. Sew one end of the tube shut.
9. Turn the tube right side out. Stuff it lightly with fiberfill.

10. Sew or glue the tube to the body to make an arm. Repeat for second arm.
11. For the legs and lower torso, repeat the same process with a different colored fabric. You can make two legs—or one long skirt. If you choose to make a skirt, tie it tightly around the "waist" of the soap bottle with another ribbon or braid. Make sure that the skirt is long and swings freely. This helps your puppet to move and dance.

Now you have puppets and a story. All you need to find is an audience!

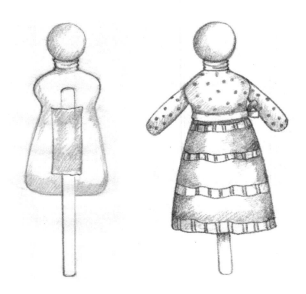

Learn a Little Spanish!

música (MOO-zee-kah): music

el teatro (ell tay-AH-tro): theater

el cine (ell SEE-nay): movie

pintar (peen-TAHR): to paint

dibujar (dee-boo-HAHR): to draw

cantar (kahn-TAHR): to sing

tocar el gitarro (toe-CAR ell gi-TAHR-roe): to play the guitar

el titere (ell TEE-tare-ay): puppet

A Honduran girl works in her family's *milpa*. Children share in the family work as soon as they are old enough to do so.
Courtesy of Nancy Black and Mary C. Turck

7

Daily Grind: Corn and Coffee

After school years are over, work takes center stage. In Mexico and Central America, unemployment runs high. Jobs of any kind can be hard to find. This chapter introduces workers from coffee farmers to factory workers sewing blue jeans.

Diego

Diego lives in a two-room house. His parents and four sisters live there, too. Their home is in San Sebastian Lemoa. Lemoa is a small town in Guatemala. A few hundred people live in the town. Hundreds more come to town on market days. They come from scattered farms.

Francisco Rivera, Diego's father, is seldom at home. He works in a big city. He can only visit his family a few times a year.

Diego and his mother and sisters work, too. They raise food for the family. They tend the *milpa* (MEEL-pah). The *milpa* seems like a very big garden or a very small farm. The family *milpa* is about 1 mile (1.6 km) from their home. Their grandparents live next to the *milpa*. The *milpa* has been in their family for generations.

Corn, beans, and squash grow together. The children help to plant. They also help with weeding or cleaning the field. The family also raises peas and potatoes. A raspberry bush, a lime tree, and two apple trees grow in the *milpa*.

All the work is done by hand. People have farmed this way for centuries. They carefully tend small fields to produce food. Even at seven years old, Diego has his own machete. He can use the long knife to cut corn. His older sisters use the hoe to loosen the soil. Diego is not yet old enough to use the big hoe.

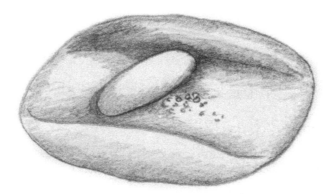

Corn is a basic food in Mexico and Central America. Diego's family raises it the same way their great-great-grandparents did. First, they clear and loosen the soil. Then, they plant the seeds. As the corn grows, they weed around it. This keeps weeds from

Making Tortillas

Some tortillas are made from corn; others are made from flour. Machines make the tortillas sold in big stores. Rural women make tortillas by hand. All day long, women are *tortillando* (tor-tee-AHN-doe), patting tortillas from one hand to the other. The rhythm of their work is everywhere.

People eat tortillas in all of Mexico and Central America. Tortillas are a basic food, just as bread is in the United States. Tortillas with salt for breakfast. Tortillas with beans for lunch. Tortillas with more beans, and maybe some cheese, for supper. Tortillas made by hand by *Mama*. Tortillas sold by women on the sidewalk in the city. Tortillas made fresh in the restaurant. Tortillas cooked over a wood fire.

You can make tortillas at home.

Materials

Adult assistance
   suggested
Mixing bowl
Measuring cups

2 cups (500 ml) *masa* (Fresh *masa* is sold in Latin American groceries. Dry *masa* is available at most supermarkets.)
1 to 1½ cups (250 to 375 ml) water (depending on humidity)
Flour
Large, cast-iron griddle or frying pan (a nonstick skillet can be used as a substitute pan)
Cooking oil or nonstick cooking spray
Wide spatula
Butter, salt, black beans (optional)

1. In a mixing bowl, moisten the *masa* with water. If you start with dry *masa*, you will need at least 1 cup (250 ml) of water. Mix thoroughly with your hands. The dough should hold together well. If it is crumbly, add a little more water. If it is too soupy, add more *masa*.
2. After mixing, let the dough rest for five minutes. The resting time is important. It makes the dough easier to handle and a little less sticky. Then, make a ball of dough about 1 inch (2.5 cm) in diameter.
3. Pat the ball back and forth between your hands. Pat it until it is flat and thin. If the mixture sticks to your hands, then sprinkle a bit of flour on your dry, clean hands in your second attempt.
4. Cook this ball, your tortilla, on a hot, cast-iron griddle or frying pan. First, heat the griddle on medium-high heat. Put your tortilla on the hot griddle. (People in Central America don't add oil when they cook tortillas, but you may want to coat the pan very lightly with cooking oil or nonstick spray.) Wait until the tortilla browns slightly on one side. Use a wide spatula to turn it. Cooking will take approximately two minutes. The exact time for cooking depends on how thick the tortilla is and the heat of the griddle.

Enjoy your tortillas with a little butter and salt, or with black beans!

You can also make tortillas from flour and water.

You can make great lunches from your own tortillas or store-bought tortillas. You can roll up beans and cheese inside a tortilla. You can sprinkle the tortilla with sugar and cinnamon for a dessert. You can bake or fry the tortilla, and then break it into chips. Tortillas are a very versatile food.

3 servings

stealing water or nutrients from the growing corn. Sometimes, children chase hungry birds away from the field of corn.

When the corn is ripe, the family picks it. Carefully, they take the kernels off the corncob. The dry kernels can be stored all year. Some will be used for seed next year. Most will become food for the family—*tortillas* (tor-TEE-ahs); *tamales* (tah-MAH-lace); *pozol* (poe-SOLE), a cornmeal soup; *atole* (ah-TOHL-ay), a drink made from cornmeal; and many other foods.

Masa (MAH-sah) is the basis for most of the corn foods. *Masa* is made by soaking or cooking corn in lime and water until it is softened. Then, it is ground. Some people still grind it the old way. They use two stones. One stone is flat or shaped like a shallow bowl. The corn is placed on this stone. A second stone is used to pound or grind it. This is very hard work!

Today, most people take the corn to a *molina* (moe-LEE-nah), or mill. The *molina* has a motor, and so it grinds corn much faster. People must give a portion of the ground corn to the *molina* owner as payment for this grinding service.

While corn, rice, and beans are very traditional foods in Central America, food is becoming more and more international. Some restaurants in Costa Rica offer a choice of rice or *espaguetti* (pasta) with meals. United States soft-drink brands, such as Coca-Cola and Pepsi Cola, are everywhere. Sometimes they are sold in bottles. Sometimes street vendors sell them in plastic bags. People bite a small hole in a corner of the bag and drink as they walk down the street or ride a bus!

Bread, too, has spread south from the United States. Bread is made from wheat, which grows better in the United States than in Mexico or Central America. (That is why corn tortillas, not bread, were traditionally eaten with every meal.) But today, many people prefer bread, even though it costs more than corn tortillas.

Cooking Gallopinto

People enjoy rice and beans in many countries. Sometimes the rice and beans are eaten separately; sometimes they are mixed together. People eat black beans, pinto beans, red beans, white beans—every possible kind of beans. In each country, people claim that the beans grown there are better than beans grown in the next country.

In Costa Rica, they prepare *gallopinto* (gah-yo-PEEN-toh). *Gallopinto* means "painted rooster." A little song celebrates *gallopinto*. The song says:

El gallopinto no pinta; (ell gah-yo-PEEN-toh no PEEN-tah)

El que pinta es el pintor! (ell kay PEEN-tah ays ell peen-TOR)

It means:

The painted rooster does not paint;

The one who paints is the painter!

As a food, however, *gallopinto* has nothing to do with roosters!

Materials

Adult assistance suggested
Measuring cups
Measuring spoons
Pot or kettle
Long-grain white rice (about 1 cup [250 ml] dry, or 3 cups [750 ml] cooked)
2 cups (500 ml) water
Large serving spoon
6 to 8 green onions
Sharp knife
Bunch of cilantro
1 can of black beans (14 to 16 ounces [875 ml to 1 l])
Sieve or colander
2 tablespoons (30 ml) butter or margarine
Frying pan

1. Combine one cup of dry rice with the water. Bring to a boil, then turn it down to simmer. Stir the rice once. Cover the pot and let it cook until all the water is absorbed. This usually takes about 15 minutes.
2. Wash and chop the green onions.
3. Wash the cilantro. Remove the leaves from the stems. Throw away the stems.
4. Empty the can of black beans into the colander. Rinse them well, until all the gooey sauce is gone.
5. Melt the butter in the frying pan. Add the onions and fry them for about two minutes, stirring frequently.
6. Add the beans and rice. Stir to mix them together.
7. When everything is hot, turn the stove off. Stir in the cilantro leaves.

Serve and enjoy!

6 servings

Agribusiness Arrives

Riding on a bus, one can see the old and new ways of farming in Guatemala. The contrasts are similar across Mexico and Central America. There is an old woman gathering sticks for firewood. A boy is holding a rope tied to a pig as the pig grazes. A girl walks behind three cows, watching over them. They represent the old ways of farming. Up on the mountain, tiny green patches show one-family farms.

But here is a large, fenced pasture with a whole herd of cows. They belong to a large rancher. Fields of snow peas, cauliflower, cabbage, broccoli, and coriander grow on the hillsides. In one, three men spray pesticides to kill insects and weeds. They wear no masks or gloves or hats. They carry the tanks of poison on their backs. In the very next field, women harvest broccoli. These crops will not feed Guatemalans. They will be shipped to U.S. markets.

These fields do not belong to the people working in them. They belong to agribusinesses. (*Agribusiness* means a very large farm-ing operation, in contrast to a family-operated farm.) Some large agribusinesses are owned by Guatemalans, or by people from the country in which they operate. Others are owned by large corporations with headquarters in foreign countries. These large businesses can take the food produced in the fields and ship it overseas to sell it.

Small farmers have a hard time making money. They have to sell their products close to home. They do not have trucks to ship it to the airport or connections to sell it in other countries. They usually grow food for their own families and to sell in local markets. They carry their products to markets in a nearby town. Then, they sell directly to the people who live in the town.

Bananas

Bananas grow on large plantations. So do pineapples. Chiquita and Dole and other large companies grow bananas and pineapples. Sometimes they own the land. Sometimes they have contracts to buy the bananas from the owners. Honduras produces the most bananas,

but other countries also have some plantations on the Atlantic Coast.

Banana workers live on the plantations. On one plantation, their homes are made of cement. They are built in long rows. Each is connected to the next. Each home is a single room, about 10 feet square (3 m sq). Each building houses a family. They sleep on the floor or on mats they make or bring with them. Workers are very poor. One worker said, "Even if I could afford a table or a bed, I'd have to leave it outside, because there's no room inside to put anything."

Field workers often work from six o'clock in the morning until eight at night. Some earn only about $40 per week. Many women work in banana-packing plants. They earn even less.

In Costa Rica, some farmers are trying a different way of raising bananas. Arnaldo is a 47-year-old farmer. He lives on the Talamanca Bribri Reserve with his wife, six children, and two grandchildren. They grow *organic* bananas. That means they grow the fruit without using any pesticides.

Arnaldo sells his bananas through the Association of Small Producers of Talamanca. The association brings together many small farmers. It gives them a way to market and a better price for their bananas. Every two weeks, Arnaldo carries his bananas through the forest to a meeting place. There, he loads the bananas onto a horse. Someone takes the horse and bananas to a road and on to market. Then, a U.S. company buys the bananas to make baby food.

Coffee

Some small farmers grow coffee. They carefully tend the coffee trees, which take two or three years to produce their first crop. Coffee trees sometimes look more like large bushes. Often farmers plant coffee under larger trees. The larger trees shade the coffee plants from intense sun. They also provide homes for birds and other wildlife. This is called a "bird friendly" coffee farm. Many small farmers grow their coffee organically.

Food for Fun—Chocobananas!

Chocobananas are a favorite snack or dessert in Honduras. In cities, street vendors sell small packets of chocobanana mix. Sometimes you can find the same mix in U.S. stores. If not, melted chocolate chips work just as well.

Materials

Adult assistance suggested
6 bananas
Craft sticks
Wax paper
Double-boiler kettle or microwave
1 package chocolate chips
Spoon or small measuring cup

1. Peel the bananas. Carefully put a stick in the end of each banana. Wrap each in wax paper. Freeze them solid.

2. Melt the chocolate chips in a microwave or in a double boiler on the stove. (A double boiler is a two-kettle arrangement, with boiling water in the bottom kettle and the chocolate in the top kettle.) Be sure not to get ANY water in the melting chocolate. You should definitely have adult assistance or supervision for melting the chocolate.

3. Hold a banana over the pan of melted chocolate. Use a spoon or small measuring cup to pour the chocolate over the banana. Work quickly! The chocolate will harden when it touches the frozen banana. Repeat with each banana.

Now you are ready to enjoy your chocobananas! Or you can wrap them in wax paper and store them in the freezer to eat another day.

6 servings

Coffee trees blossom during the rainy season. The blossoms produce bright red coffee cherries. Farmers pick the cherries when they have grown for several months. Then, they spread the cherries out to dry in the sun. While the cherries are drying, the farmers turn them over often to expose them to the sun. Drying takes two to three weeks.

After the coffee cherries are dry, two more steps remain. The red, pulpy outer covering must be removed. Then, the gray-green coffee bean must be roasted. Coffee roasters are large, expensive machines. Small farmers cannot afford these machines. So they sell their coffee beans to big companies. The big companies ship the beans to Europe and the United States.

Large companies also own large coffee plantations. About 300,000 Guatemalans work full-time on coffee plantations. They usually live in shacks with dirt floors. They have little protection from pesticides in the fields. They earn even less than the banana workers do.

The coffee harvest runs from November to January. During this time, more workers are needed. Some 375,000 temporary workers arrive. Most of them come from their own small farms. They grow corn and other

food on their own farms, but they cannot grow enough to make a living. So they travel to do temporary work to provide more income to help support their family. Whole families may work together in the fields. Children help parents pick coffee beans. Many farm workers can no longer find jobs. Many move to the cities to look for work.

World prices for coffee and bananas are low. Sometimes farmers organize in cooperatives to get better prices.

Coffee is grown in most countries of Central America and also in Mexico. Mut Vitz is a coffee growing cooperative in southern Mexico. Mut Vitz coffee growers agree not to use chemicals on their land. Their coffee is all shade-grown, or "bird-friendly." Lucio Gonzalez Ruiz explains how the Mut Vitz coffee cooperative began, and how it works:

We started to organize this cooperative or association of coffee producers for several reasons. The main reason is that we have to deal with middlemen, called "coyotes." They set the price for our coffee and the manner of payment; they cheat us when they weigh the coffee; they won't pay the full price because they claim the coffee is not dry or it is spotted. Right now the price for coffee is extremely low. . . .

We also have expenses: we pay workers for helping at harvest time. Landless *campesinos* or those who come from areas where there is no coffee come to help us with the harvest. But we hardly can make it with the little price we get for our coffee. . . .

We decided that it was better to form an association and to try our luck exporting our coffee in the fair-trade market. We formed a board of directors and thought of names. We decided to call the cooperative Mut Vitz, because our meeting place is at the foothills of the highest mountain in the region, called *Mut Vitz*. This mountain is a resting place for thousands of migratory birds that fly in from the north during the months of October and November. Our grandparents used to celebrate the arrival of the birds and they named this mountain Mut Vitz, which in Tzotzil means "Bird Mountain." So, we named our association Mut Vitz.

In March 1999, after our '98–'99 harvest, we had our first export sale. We sold a container of coffee to two buyers in the United States: Half a container to each buyer. This was good for us, it helped the cooperative and it helped the producers. At this time the price for coffee in Bochil was of 12 pesos ($1) a kilogram (2.2 lb), and Mut Vitz paid the producers the guaranteed price of 18 pesos ($1.60) a kilogram.

Working in the *Maquila*

A *maquiladora* (MAH-keel-ah-DOHR-ah) is a factory that makes goods to export. *Maquila* (MAH-keel-ah) is a short name for *maquiladora*. Many *maquilas* are located close to each other. Some are in or near big cities. Others are near the United States–Mexico border.

Other countries have *maquilas*, too. El Salvador, Nicaragua, and Honduras have all created special *maquila* zones. These are places set aside for factories producing for export. The governments want *maquila* factories to come to their countries. They lower taxes for *maquilas* in the special zones.

Elena's work

Elena works at a Mexican *maquila* called *Cantabria*:

"I earn 224 pesos (US$28) a week and work Monday–Friday from 8 A.M. until 6 P.M. or 7 P.M. We get a half-hour lunch break at 1 P.M. I've been working there for about two years. Saturdays we enter at 8 A.M. and the exit time is 2 P.M. They don't give us a break on Saturdays, not even to eat. And when they have a lot of work to finish, we don't leave sometimes until 4 P.M. on Saturdays.

"After we've finished our daily production quotas, if they reject any of our work, we have to stay after until we finish all the repairs. This usually ends up meaning that we leave after 8 P.M., sometimes not until 10 P.M. When I leave at 10:00 at night, they pay me the same amount because they say that the repairs are our fault and we have to fix them because we didn't do the work well.

"If there's something the matter with the stitching, we have to sew them by hand to fix them. So only when we finish with all of the repairs can we leave, we can't leave earlier because they won't give us our ID's."

Unions: Promise and Peril

How can workers get better wages and conditions? They organize unions. If one worker demands better wages, she may get fired. If all the workers demand better wages, the employer is more likely to listen. If the employer does not listen, the workers go out on *strike*. This means they stop working to put pressure on the employer. When workers stick together, the union is more powerful than an individual because if all workers strike, no work is done and the business will be shut down.

Some employers talk with unions. They arrive at agreements that take into consideration both the workers' and the employers' needs. They sign a contract. This is called *collective bargaining*.

Other employers fight against unions. They refuse to negotiate. They fire workers who join unions. Sometimes even worse things happen.

Lucia Caballero

Lucia Caballero worked at a *maquila* in Honduras in 2003. She tried to organize a union. The *maquila* owners did not want a union. They threatened to close the factory. A security guard attacked Lucia. She tried to leave the *maquila* to get medical help. The *maquila* fired Lucia for leaving without permission. They did nothing to the security guard who attacked her.

You Can Work for Change

Many people around the world want to improve working conditions in *maquilas*, or sweatshops. (*Sweatshop* is a name used for factories that treat workers unfairly.) And there are things that kids and other consumers can do to help support companies that treat workers fairly and thereby encourage other companies to change their practices. Here are a few organizations that are involved in these efforts:

- **The Clean Clothes Campaign** (www.cleanclothes.org) organizes consumers to send postcards to companies with questions about working conditions. Consumers pressure companies to use their influence to improve working conditions. They do not want companies to just close factories where there are problems.

- **No Sweat** (www.nosweatpparel.com) is a for-profit company that buys clothing only from factories with unions. For example, they buy from the Mexmode factory in Mexico. Workers there succeeded in organizing a union in 2001. The United Students Against Sweatshops supported the workers in organizing a union.

- **The Sweat Free Schools Campaign** (www.labor-religion.org/sweatfreetop.htm) helps junior high- and high-school students organize in their school districts. They want school district money to go to companies that treat workers fairly. They ask school districts to buy only sweat-free athletic equipment and clothing.

May 1 Is Labor Day Around the World

On May 1, Labor Day, workers around the world celebrate unions. They celebrate the rights they have won. They celebrate solidarity with other workers. In many cities, they march and hold rallies. They plan to win better wages and working conditions. In the United States, Labor Day is celebrated on the first Monday in September.

The Union, A Stage Play

Characters

Estela, a worker with three children
Fernando, her husband
Dori, friend and coworker
Rosa, union organizer
Other workers
Supervisor
Guard 1
Guard 2
Police officer 1
Police officer 2

Props

Scraps of material and thread
Shirts
2 (or more) sewing machines
Clipboard
Pencil
Sweaters and purses
Cards
Tables
Chairs
Bowls
Spoons
Check
Telephone
Crutches

Scene I: In the Factory

The stage is divided into two parts: the left half is the factory; the right half is the street outside. Two armed, uniformed guards stand outside the factory door, on the street side. On the factory side, workers are crowded together. Each is sitting hunched over a sewing machine sewing on the shirt. More shirts are stacked near each sewing machine. If possible, sewing machines are running, making noise. Scraps of material and thread litter the stage. Dori and Elena are sewing at machines at the front of the stage. The supervisor enters from stage left. He is wearing a suit or uniform, with a name badge. He carries a clipboard and pencil.

Supervisor: Estela, you are not sewing fast enough. You still have shirts to finish from yesterday. You will have to work until your quota is finished.

Estela: But, sir, I worked late last night.

Supervisor: If you want your job, you will finish your quota—tonight. If you don't finish, don't bother coming back tomorrow.

Estela: My baby is sick. I need to go home to take care of her.

Supervisor: If your baby is sick, you need your job to pay for the doctor.

(Supervisor exits stage left.)

(Estela looks as if she is about to cry. She wipes her eyes on her sleeve.)

Dori: Don't worry, *amiga*. I'll help you.

Estela: But you have your work.

Dori: I only have a few shirts to finish. I can help you, too.

(The other workers get up and leave their machines. They go through the door, past the guards, and off the stage. They should improvise parting conversations—see you tomorrow, have a nice evening, etc. Estela and Dori bend over their machines, sewing as fast as they can. The lights go out. Then the lights come back on—they are finally done! Now Estela and Dori gather their purses and sweaters and leave. As they leave, the guards turn out the lights on the factory half. Rosa falls into step with Estela and Dori. The guards watch suspiciously.)

Rosa: (in a stage whisper) Have you heard about the union? We are trying to organize the workers here. I have cards to sign. If enough workers sign the cards, we can have an election for the union.

Estela: Give me a card. I will take it home and talk to my husband.

Dori: Be careful, Estela. You could get in trouble.

Rosa: We need to stand together. If we are united, we can stand up to the bosses.

(Rosa gives them each a card as they leave the stage.)

Scene II: At Home

Fernando and Estela are sitting at the table with bowls of beans or soup.

Fernando: The baby is getting a little better. My mother said she didn't cough so much today.

Estela: I am glad your mother can take care of her while we work. I would hate to leave her with a stranger.

Fernando: *Mama* loves having babies in the house.

Estela: I am so tired.

Fernando: This is the third night this week you had to work late.

Estela: Yes—and look at this check. I didn't get any pay for overtime.

Fernando: They work you so hard, and then don't even pay for it.

Estela: A girl was talking to us after we left. She said the union is organizing. See—I brought this card home.

Fernando: It would be good to have a union behind you. Then the company would have to follow the law on overtime.

Estela: Dori said we could get in trouble if we sign the cards.

Fernando: That's true. The bosses don't like unions. But I think the union is a good thing. We need help to stand up to the company.

Estela: I think I am going to sign this time. I don't want trouble, but I want my rights.

Scene III: Outside the Factory at Lunchtime

Rosa sits and talks with Estela, Dori, and a few other women. The two guards watch suspiciously.

Guard 1: (speaking to Rosa) You—what are you doing here?

Rosa: I'm just talking with friends.

Guard 2: This is a factory, not a bar. Get off this property.

Rosa: The factory is behind the gate. This is a public street and a public sidewalk.

Guard 1: You heard him. Get out. The company owns this property.

Dori: Go, Rosa, please. We don't want trouble.

Rosa: If you say so. But I will be back.

Scene IV: Outside the Factory at Lunchtime the Next Day

Rosa is on crutches. The guards are at the gate. They snicker and point at Rosa. Four women cluster around her and talk.

Dori: Rosa, what happened to you?

Rosa: Ah, last night someone followed me. They grabbed me and beat me up. They said I had to leave the union. Stop causing trouble.

Estela: But Rosa, that's terrible! You should call the police!

Rosa: The police always take the side of the company.

Dori: Aren't you afraid to come back here?

Rosa: I'm not going to let them scare me off.

(The supervisor comes out and stands in the doorway, telephone in hand. Two police officers approach.)

Police Officer 1: You are under arrest.

Rosa: What are the charges?

Police Officer 1: Trespassing on private property.

Estela: But this is the public sidewalk!

Police Officer 2: Watch out, or you will be in trouble, too.

(The police drag Rosa away. The supervisor goes to the women.)

Supervisor: Get to work. You don't have time to stand around talking.

(The women start to go in.)

Supervisor: Estela. Dori. Not you. You have been talking to that union troublemaker. You're fired.

(The women turn around and watch.)

Estela: You can't fire us for talking!

Dori: We have our rights!

Supervisor: You're fired, both of you. Just count yourselves lucky that I didn't call the cops for you, too.

Worker 1: You can't fire them. They didn't do anything.

Worker 2: That's right. We have a right to talk to anyone we want.

Supervisor: Anyone who wants unions wants trouble.

Worker 1: Then maybe we have trouble right now. Come on, *amigas*! Let's strike!

Estela: Yes—let's strike right now!

Worker 2: (calls into the factory) They beat up Rosa! They fired Estela and Dori! On strike now!

(Women march out of the factory and turn out the lights. They link arms and stand, facing the audience. The supervisor stands off to the side, pretending to talk into his cell phone.)

Together, the women chant, five times:

The people, united,
Will never be defeated.

(or

*El pueblo, unido,
jamas será vencido!*)

Questions for Further Discussion

1. Why does Rosa want a union?

2. Who do you think followed Rosa? Why?

3. What does it mean to go on strike? Do you think the workers will support Dori and Estela by going on strike? Would you? Why or why not?

Learn a Little Spanish!

trabajo (trah-BAH-ho): work

maquiladora (MAH-keel-ah-DOHR-ah): factory that makes goods for export

velado (vay-LAH-doe): overnight, overtime work

arroz (ah-ROSE): rice

pollo (POY-oh): chicken

carne (CAR-nay): meat

frijoles (free-HO-lase): beans

maíz (my-EES): corn

milpa (MEEL-pah): cornfield

molina (moh-LEE-nah): mill

tortillas (tor-TEE-ahs): flat, pancakelike food made from corn or flour

tamales (tah-MAH-lace): ground corn, stuffed with beans or other filling, wrapped in a corn husk

pozol (poe-SOLE): puddinglike food made of ground corn

atole (ah-TOHL-ay): drink made from corn

masa (MAH-sah): ground corn dough

Of course, work isn't everything in life! In the next chapter, celebrations take center stage.

This band rides on a float in a parade going through San Pedro Sula for one of the many Honduran celebrations. *Courtesy of Mary C. Turck*

Celebrating Life

This chapter focuses on celebrations of special events in the lives of people and families. A Maya family celebrates the birth of a child. Children break a *piñata* for a birthday party. Godparents help to guide young married couples. You'll find these celebrations and more in the pages that follow.

Born in the Mountains

Slowly, a woman walks up the mountain road in the Guatemalan highlands. Her large belly shows a baby is coming. She speaks quietly. No one is with her. She is talking to the baby inside her. "This is *maíz* (my-EES; corn) in the field. *Maíz* is our life. You are made of *maíz*. You grow when I eat *maíz*. When you grow older, you will tend the fields. You will always show respect for the *maíz*. You will show respect for all nature."

Every day, the woman speaks to her unborn child. As she works in the field, she explains her work. As she grinds *maíz* for tortillas, she tells the child what she is doing. She continues with her work. The child needs to learn about daily work. The mother has begun to teach the Maya way of life.

No one eats in front of the pregnant woman, unless they share food with her. It would be disrespectful to eat without feeding the woman and her growing baby. All

the time she is pregnant, the community helps her.

Finally, the day of birth arrives. A village leader is with the parents. Usually, she is a midwife to help with the birth. Two other couples come, too. They may be the grandparents. If the grandparents are not near, other couples take their places. They will welcome the baby into the community. Birth is not just a matter for mothers, or even for mothers and fathers. Birth is important to the whole community. The baby is a new member of the community.

The mother and baby rest for eight days. No other children can visit them. Neighbors bring small gifts and food for the mother.

After eight days, the whole house is cleaned. Children and other family members welcome the mother and baby. They light four candles around the bed to represent the four corners of the house that is their home. They give the baby a little bag containing garlic, lime, salt, and tobacco. Tobacco and

Papel Picado

Papel picado (pah-PELL pee-CAH-do) means "cut paper." In some countries, it is called *papel de seda* (pah-PELL de SAY-da), or silk paper, because it looks like delicate silk. In Mexico, it is sometimes called *papel de China*, or Chinese paper, because the first tissue paper in Mexico came from China in the 16th century. By whatever name, *papel picado* makes a bright, festive decoration. The sheets are displayed on strings that run across rooms or churches or even streets.

Materials

12 x 18 inch (30 x 46 cm) sheets of tissue
    paper, bright colors
Scissors
String
Glue or tape

1. Fold a sheet of tissue paper in half, then in half again.
2. Cut designs into the folded edges. You can make scallops (half circles), diamonds, or squares.
3. Unfold the paper and look at it. If you like it, you can leave it as it is. If not, refold it and cut some more designs.
4. You can make fancier designs. If you cut half of a flower, the whole flower will appear when the paper is unfolded. Experiment!
5. After you have cut several papers into designs, fold them in half and hang across the string. Attach the string to walls or windows with tape.

You can also use square-shaped pieces of tissue paper, folding them on the diagonal, to make triangle shapes that can be hung over the top of the string.

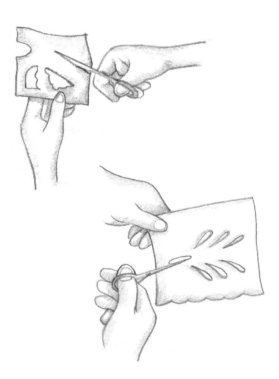

lime are sacred to Mayas. The bag represents traditions.

After 40 days, the baby is a full member of the community. This calls for another celebration. Perhaps the baby will now be baptized. People will eat a meal together and celebrate the new member of the community.

Baptism

Many people living in Mexico and Central America are Catholics. In this religion, babies are baptized. (*Baptism* is a religious ceremony that includes pouring water and saying prayers over the baby.) Baptism makes the child part of the religious community.

Baptism often takes place in a church, though it can be done at home. Families in rural areas may wait a long time for baptism. Sometimes a priest or religious leader visits their town only a few times a year. Sometimes they need to travel a long distance to a town with a church.

Before the baptism, the parents choose godparents for the baby. The godparents are called the *comadre* (ko-MAH-dray) and *compadre* (kohm-PAH-dray). The godparents are people who promise to help the parents raise the child. Godparents may be relatives, such as aunts and uncles, or those not related but who become part of the family. Godparents and their families may celebrate holidays together. Godparents may help with school expenses when the child is older. They give gifts to the child on birthdays. They give advice to the parents. They will be an important part of the child's life.

For the baptism, everyone dresses in his or her best clothes. The baby may wear a special dress, passed down from parents and grandparents. Traditionally, priests perform baptisms. Today, other religious leaders, such as nuns, may do so. At the baptism, the religious leader pours water over the baby's head or even lowers the baby into a large container of water.

The religious leader speaks the ritual words, welcoming the child to the church community and giving the child his or her name. This may be different than the name

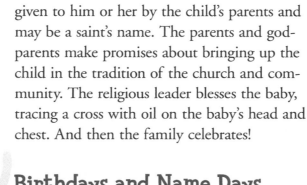

given to him or her by the child's parents and may be a saint's name. The parents and godparents make promises about bringing up the child in the tradition of the church and community. The religious leader blesses the baby, tracing a cross with oil on the baby's head and chest. And then the family celebrates!

Birthdays and Name Days

¡Feliz Cumpleaños! (fay-LEES COOM-play-AHN-yose): Happy Birthday! Parties, presents, and *piñatas* make birthdays special in any country.

In Mexico and Central America, people may celebrate another special day. This is a child's name day. The *name day* is the day dedicated to a saint. Many Catholic children are named after saints. For example, a girl might be named Teresa. Catholics remember two special saints with this name. Teresa of Avila was a holy and wise woman. She lived in Spain in the 16th century. Her special day is October 15. Therese of Lisieux was a humble and kind young woman. She died

when she was only 24 years old. She lived in France in the 19th century. Her special day is October 1. If your parents named you Teresa, you or they will choose one of these saints as "your" saint. Then you could celebrate her special day each year.

Quinceañera

A girl's fifteenth birthday is special in Mexico and most Central American countries. Now she is *quince* (KEEN-say)—15 years old. She is ready to become a woman. She is also ready to celebrate with a special party—her *quinceañera* (KEEN-say-ahn-YARE-ah). Sometimes the name of the party is shortened to *quince*.

Let's look in on a *quinceañera* party. The young woman celebrating *quince* is dressed in a beautiful formal dress. She looks almost like a bride! In fact, everyone is beautifully dressed, as if this were a wedding. The *quince*'s father wears a tuxedo. So do some of the young men. Her mother and the young women wear formal dresses.

Making *Piñatas*

Piñatas make any celebration more fun! The *piñata* may look like an animal or some other shape. It hangs from a tree or from the ceiling. A grown up holds the rope that is tied to the *piñata*. She pulls the rope to swing the *piñata* up and down and around. A blindfolded child swings a stick or bat. She tries to break the *piñata*. The other children stand in a circle. They laugh and cheer and wait for their turn to hit the *piñata*. We hope they are far from the swinging stick!

When the *piñata* breaks, candy falls out of it. The candy scatters across the floor and all the children scramble for it.

Some people claim that *piñatas* came from Spain to Mexico. They say the first *piñatas* were brought to Spain by Marco Polo. He brought the idea back from China, where people celebrated the new year by breaking *piñatas*.

Others insist that *piñatas* came from the Aztecs. Aztec priests decorated clay *piñatas* with feathers and filled them with little treasures. These *piñatas* were broken to celebrate the birthday of Huitzilopochtli (weet-see-lo-POCHT-lee), the god of war.

Traditionally, Mexicans celebrate Christmas with *piñatas*. The Christmas *piñatas* are filled with candies, fruit, and more, including guavas, oranges, sugarcane, and peanuts. Often, little baskets of candy are kept ready to pass around after the *piñata* breaks, so that children who don't get close enough to grab candy will not be disappointed.

Materials

Large balloons
String
Clotheslines, shower rod, or tree branch
  (optional)
Newspapers
Ruler
Mixing bowl
Flour
Water
Scissors
Wrapped candy
Tape
Tissue paper, colorful
Glue

1. Blow up the balloons and tie strings to the ends. If you can hang them from a doorway, clothes line, shower rod, or tree branch, that's great. It makes the next steps easier.

2. Tear the newspaper into 1-inch (2.5-cm) wide strips. The strips should be about 10 inches (25 cm) long for easy handling. If you are working indoors, spread extra newspapers over your work surface to keep it clean. If the balloons are hanging, spread newspapers under them, too.

3. In a mixing bowl, mix equal parts flour and water to make a thin, goopy, sticky paste.

4. Dip each strip of newspaper into the flour-water paste. Use your fingers to squeeze off the extra paste. Then, wrap the newspaper strip around a balloon. Repeat until each balloon is completely covered with two or three layers of newspaper.

5. Next, decide what kind of *piñata* you are making. After the balloons dry, you could put two of them together to make a person or an animal. You could also make smaller shapes completely out of the paper and paste, and then attach them to the balloon with more paper and paste. Or you could just decorate a one-balloon *piñata*. This is the time to decide and to make enough balloons and other shapes out of your paper and paste.

6. Now comes the hard part. You have to wait for the *piñatas* and any other pieces you have made to dry *completely*. This may take a day or more.

7. Once your *piñatas* are dry, if you are putting pieces together, you can do that now. Usually, paper and paste works better than glue in keeping the pieces together.

8. If you want to fill your *piñata* with candy, now is the time. Carefully cut a small hole in the top. Pour in wrapped pieces of candy. (Remember, it will all fall on the floor!) Replace the piece of *piñata* that you cut out to make the hole, and tape it in place.

9. Choose the colors you want to use to decorate your *piñatas*. Cut the tissue paper into strips that are 3 inches (7.5 cm) wide and 15 inches (38 cm) long. You will need a lot of strips to cover the *piñata* completely.

10. Fold each strip of tissue paper in half, so the two long sides are together. Make cuts about 1 inch (2.5 cm) deep and ⅜-inch (.75-cm) apart all along the fold. This will make a nice ruffle.

11. Glue the ruffled paper to the *piñata*. Place one row close to the next. Make nice, even rows of paper until you have covered the *piñata* completely.

Congratulations! You and your *piñata* are ready to party!

Before the party, they all go to church. There are special prayers for the young lady on her special day. The prayers ask God's blessing on her as she takes her place in the world of grown-ups. Then, they go to a hall for the party.

Tables are loaded with food. A band plays and the young people look ready to dance. The first dance is a waltz. The *quince* and her proud father lead the dance. After the first dance is over, everyone wants to dance with her!

The *quince* (used to refer to both the party and the young lady) dances all night. She is no longer a little girl. Now she is a woman! But the next morning, *Mamí* (Mommy) wakes her. To her family, she is still a child. She still has dishes to wash and homework to finish!

Many girls do not have special *quince* parties. The parties are expensive. Many families cannot afford them. Some believe it is more important to save money for education, or to help those who are less fortunate.

Weddings

Getting married is a festive event all over the world. As time goes on, many of the old customs fade away. A big-city boy may propose to his girlfriend. They decide when and how they will marry. But in some families, especially in rural areas, old traditions remain.

Mothers or aunts chaperone young women, so they do not spend time alone with young men. In a rural community in Honduras, the *paseo* (pah-SAY-oh), or procession, offers a time to meet. In the evening, families go to the town square. Young women walk around the square in one direction. Young men walk around in the opposite direction. Sometimes they stop to talk and giggle. They get to know each other slowly.

When a young man wants to propose, he goes to the young woman's father. He first tells the father that he would like to marry his daughter. Both families are involved in the proposal. The wedding is not just

between two young people, but between their families. It will affect their whole community.

In Mexico, many people have two weddings. First, they are married under the law. They go to the courthouse or registrar and sign all the papers. Then, they are married in church. The church wedding is usually more festive. That's when people have a party!

For the church wedding, many couples have godparents. The *padrino* (pa-DREE-no) and *madrino* (ma-DREE-no) are like the best man and maid of honor, but they have more responsibilities. If the young couple has difficulties, they can go to the *padrinos* for help. The *padrinos* may help them to settle fights. They may give advice on life problems, too. They will remain lifelong friends of the couple.

This chapter focused on celebrations of life events for individuals and families. The next chapter looks at celebrations that take place at special times of the year.

Learn a Little Spanish!

madre (MAH-dray): mother

padre (PAH-dray): father

hija/hijo (EE-ha or EE-hoe): daughter or son

hermana/hermano (air-MAH-nah or air-MAH-noe): sister or brother

tía/tío (TEE-ah or TEE-oh): aunt or uncle

abuela/abuelo (ah-BWAY-la or ah-BWAY-loe): grandmother or grandfather

—ito (ee-toe): a suffix meaning "little;" "herman-ito" is a little brother

cumpleaños (COOM-play-AHN-yose): birthday

quinceañera (KEEN-say-ahn-YARE-ah): special celebration for a young woman's fifteenth birthday; sometimes also used to refer to the young woman who is celebrating

9

Religious and Patriotic Holidays

Though Christmas is celebrated across the Americas, some customs change from one country to the next. Each country celebrates patriotic holidays, but independence did not come on the same date to all. This chapter introduces interesting ways to celebrate, from the processions of Mexico's *Posadas* and Costa Rica's *topes* to the intricately designed *alfombras* of Guatemala.

All day long, people flood into León, Nicaragua. Some walk or take buses from nearby towns. Some return from far away to the city where they grew up. Tonight they will celebrate. Tonight is *La Gritería* (lah gree-tare-EE-ah)! It celebrates the feast day of the Blessed Virgin Mary.

La Gritería takes place on the evening of December 7. The sun sets early, and excitement is in the air. At six o'clock in the evening, fireworks begin. Every street and every block is lit by flashes and resounds with explosions.

Up and down the street, children and adults knock on doors. They go from one house to another. At each home, they ask, "*¿Qué causa tanta alegría?*"—"What causes so much happiness?"

The family inside the house shouts back the answer: "*¡La concepción de María!*"— "The conception of Mary!" The holiday celebrates the conception of Mary, the mother of Jesus.

The families in the houses give gifts to their visitors. The gifts are small, but welcome—a bag of rice and beans, an apple, and a toothbrush. The people of León are known for their generosity. That is why so many people have come to León for this night.

As the visitors leave, everyone shouts together: "*¡Qué viva la Virgen!*"—"Long live the Virgin!" By midnight, the doors are closing. A final round of fireworks marks the end of *La Gritería* for another year.

In Guatemala City, people celebrate December 7 with *Quema del Diablo* (KAY-mah dell dee-AH-blow), which means "Burning the Devil."

During the days before the holiday, people clean homes and offices. Old mattresses, clothes, and paper—all are thrown in big piles on the street. On street corners, boys sell red-devil *piñatas*. These *piñatas* are stuffed with firecrackers, not candy.

At dusk, everyone gathers in the streets. The devil *piñatas* are lit on fire and thrown into the piles of garbage. Explosions fill the air! People throw more firecrackers onto the bonfires.

As houses are cleaned and the devil is burned, Christmas celebrations begin.

Who Is the Virgin Mary?

The Blessed Virgin Mary is the mother of Jesus. She is often called simply "the Virgin." The Catholic Church teaches that she was a virgin when Jesus was born. His only father was God.

The Catholic Church believes that Mary never sinned. It teaches that all people are born sinful—except Mary. She was conceived without sin. This is called the *Immaculate Conception*. This is the holiday celebrated in *La Gritería*.

The Spanish conquistadors brought their religion with them. They forced Indians throughout Latin America to become Catholic. Catholicism is still the largest religion in Mexico and Central America. Many important holidays have religious roots.

Christmas–*Navidad*

Santa Claus? Christmas trees? Yes—United States culture has brought both to Mexico and Central America. The mixture of cultures and traditions plays out in many ways.

Traditionally, the baby Jesus is believed to bring gifts to children in Costa Rica. The three wise men bring the gifts in Mexico—and they wait until January 6.

Imported pine trees cost a lot. Cypress wreaths and garlands are more traditional. Decked with bright red coffee berries or brilliant orchids, they also say *Feliz Navidad*—Merry Christmas!

Throughout Mexico and Central America, people celebrate with *Las Posadas* (lahs poh-SAH-dahs). Groups of neighbors gather at a home. Then, they parade from house to house. They sing as they walk. They act out the journey of Mary and Joseph in Bethlehem. They ask for shelter at the *posada*, or inn. The people at the door refuse at first. Finally, they welcome the visitors. Together, they sing, pray, and enjoy special Christmas foods.

Las Posadas continue from December 16 to December 24. In Mexico, people carry statues of Mary and Joseph from house to house. A child may dress as an angel to lead the parade. In Guatemala, drummers accompany the *posadas*. People often light fireworks in celebration.

On Christmas Eve, families gather to celebrate together. They eat a festive meal, often with a lot of *tamales*. Then, they may go to church for the *Misa del Gallo* (MEE-sah dell GAH-yo). This is the "Rooster Mass" at midnight. At midnight, fireworks explode to celebrate the birth of Jesus.

Celebrations continue after December 25. In Costa Rica, grand *topes* (TOH-pays), or parades, wind through downtown streets. Fancy horses and painted oxcarts share parade space with pretty girls on floats.

Throughout the area, Christmas ends on January 6. This is the feast day of the three kings, or wise men. For many families, this is the traditional day for gift-giving.

Building a *Nacimiento*

A *nacimiento* (nah-see-mee-EN-toh) is a nativity scene. It shows Mary and Joseph and the baby Jesus in a barn or cave. Sometimes the *nacimiento* is small. It might sit under a Christmas tree or on a table. Sometimes it is large. Then it takes up part of a room, or is built in front of the house.

Costa Ricans call the scene a *portal* (pohr-TAHL). Many families build their own *portal* each year. Sometimes they use grass, moss, and colored sawdust. If a family does not own a house, they should not build their own *portal*. Instead, they set up a *portal* given to them as a gift. They hope this will bring them the blessing of a home of their own.

Materials

Several small statues or dolls—one a baby
Fabric, brown, blue, white, and red
Scissors
Needle
Thread
String
Embroidery thread
Gold braid
Cardboard box large enough to make a little house

Acrylic paints, brown and gray
Paintbrushes
Small box to make a bed for the baby
Straw or newspaper
Aluminum foil
Tape or glue
Toy cows, donkeys, and sheep

1. Traditionally, Mary wears blue and Joseph wears red or brown. The baby Jesus is wrapped in white cloth. Cut the blue and red or brown cloth into strips wide enough to make cloaks and tunics. Hold a piece of fabric next to a doll and then double that amount to find the right length to fit it. Repeat for each doll.
2. Cut a hole in the middle of each strip of cloth to make a tunic.

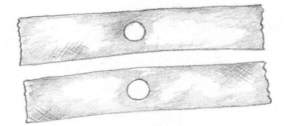

3. Sew up the sides, leaving room for the arms to come through.

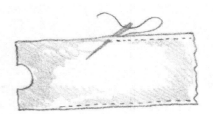

4. Tie tunics at the waist with thread or string. Wrap cloak around each person and sew or tie shut at the neck.

5. Dress additional statues as shepherds or wise men or angels. Mary and Joseph and the shepherds are dressed in very plain clothes. The angels and kings can have much fancier clothes. Decorate them with crowns or embroidery or gold braid!

6. Remove any flaps from the cardboard box

7. Make a star using the cardboard from one of the flaps.

8. Paint the inside of the box brown.

9. Paint the outside of the box with gray shapes that resemble rocks or stones.

10. Paint the smaller box brown.

11. When the big box is dry, place it on its side. This box is the stable. Fill the little box with straw. The little box is the *manger*, the place that animals eat. That is where the baby will have its bed. (If you don't have straw, cut up the newspaper into narrow strips. Use them to line the bed and floor.)

12. Wrap aluminum foil around the star that you cut from the cardboard flap in step 7.

13. Tape or glue it to the top of the stable.

14. Arrange the statues and the toy animals in the stable. An angel can stand on top of the stable. The shepherds can stand just outside the stable.

Traditionally, baby Jesus is not placed in the *nacimiento* until midnight on Christmas Eve. The wise men, or kings, are journeying from far away. They may be placed across the room, and come closer each day. They arrive on January 6. That is the last day of Christmas. Now it is time to put away the decorations and the *nacimiento* for another year.

The Christmas Story

The Christmas story is the story of the birth of Jesus. His mother, Mary, and his father (or earthly father), Joseph, travel to Bethlehem. The emperor has ordered a *census* (a count of the people), and they must go to Bethlehem to register.

Mary is pregnant. She rides a donkey. Joseph walks beside her. The journey takes days. When they arrive, they are tired. Mary is soon to give birth. But Bethlehem is filled with travelers. The couple goes from door to door. There is no room for them to sleep.

Finally, a man lets them sleep in a *stable*, or cave. This is where the family cows and oxen live. There—among the animals—Mary gives birth to Jesus.

A bright star shines overhead. Angels sing to shepherds in the fields. Soon, shepherds come to welcome the new baby. Three wise men, or kings, come from far away. They bring gifts for the baby Jesus.

Luminarias/Farolitos

Traditionally, families lit small fires outside their homes at Christmastime. The fires were to light the way for the baby Jesus. These fires were called *luminarias* (LOO-min-AHR-ee-ahs). Sometimes the fires were built on flat rooftops of *adobe* homes.

Today, fire lights small paper bags. These small fires were called *farolitos* (fahr-oh-LEE-tohs), or lanterns. Today, they may be called either *luminarias* or *farolitos*.

Materials

Adult assistance suggested
Paper bags
Scissors or hole punch
Sand
Small votive candles

1. Fold over the top of each paper bag about 1 inch (2.5 cm).
2. Make small designs in the paper bags. You can use scissors or hole punches to make the designs. Make any kind of design that you like, but be sure that the design is not too large. A large design would let the wind blow through the bag and blow out the candle. Also, be sure that you leave three inches (five cm) uncut at the bottom of the bag.
3. Fill each paper bag with at least 2 inches (7.5 cm) of sand.
4. Anchor the votive candle securely in the sand by pressing it into the sand far enough so that it is supported by the sand.
5. Set the paper bags outside to line the sidewalk (with adult permission and supervision, of course). Light the candles and enjoy your *luminarias*.

Creating an *Alfombra*

During *Semana Santa*, many families in Guatemala create *alfombras* (ahl-FOME-brahs). (*Alfombra* means "carpet.") Families use colored sawdust, flower petals, pine needles, and seeds to make *alformbras*. They create the *alfombra* in front of their home before Good Friday, the Friday of Holy Week. Then, the Good Friday procession comes down the street. Marchers carry platforms with heavy statues. People follow figures of Jesus and his disciples. The procession walks over each *alfombra*. The marching feet destroy the work of art.

The Guatemalan city of Antigua bustles with tourists during *Semana Santa*. Tourists come from all over the world to see Antigua's famous *alfombras*. Sonsonate, a city in El Salvador, also boasts of its beautiful *alfombras*. Families save all year so they can create an *alfombra*.

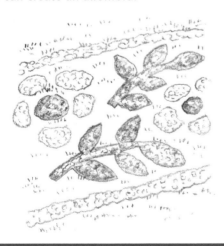

Why do people create beautiful artwork to be destroyed? The *alfombra* is a sacrifice. The creation of these is a prayer. It inspires the people who see it during the Holy Week procession. Here's your chance to create an *alfombra*, too, although yours will be much smaller than those in Antigua or Sonsonate.

Materials

Poster board

Pencil

Newspapers

Sand, black or brown and different colors

Glue or rubber cement

Chalk, various colors (optional)

1. Begin by drawing a design on the poster board using a pencil. You might draw Christian symbols, such as the cross or a lamb, or maybe you'd like to make a design that includes all the images that bring you joy during this time of year. Be sure to make a beautiful border design around the edge of your *alfombra*. You could use symbols of the season or geometric shapes and designs.

2. Decide which sand colors go in which places. Mark the places on the drawing with the color names. The poster board must be entirely covered with color.

3. Cover your work surface with newspapers.

4. Begin with brown or black sand. Carefully spread glue or rubber cement over the spaces where these colors go. Then, sprinkle the right color of sand over those spaces. Gently shake any extra sand onto the newspaper. Always start with the darkest color(s) to prevent covering up the lighter colors.

5. Repeat with each color, until you have completely filled your *alfombra* with color.

Once it's entirely dried, you can share your *alfombra* by hanging it on the wall, or setting it on a coffee table or end table.

Alternative: You can use colored chalk to create an *alfombra* outdoors. Draw your design in sidewalk squares. Just like the *alfombras* of Antigua, your sidewalk *alfombra* will be worn away by the feet of passing people.

Ojo de Dios

Ojo de dios means "eye of God." This popular decoration is often hung at Christmastime. It can be used at any time of the year.

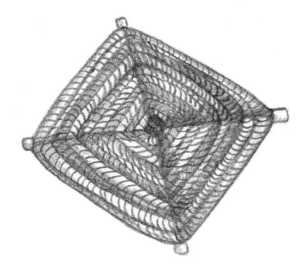

Materials

Craft sticks
Yarn, many colors
Scissors

1. Hold the sticks so that they cross in the middle. Wrap or tie the yarn to hold the sticks together.
2. Now, take the first color of yarn. Wind it in one complete turn around one of the sticks, then bring it over to the next stick. Wind it completely around that stick, and then over to the next. Work your way around the cross.

3. After you have made several rows of one color of yarn, tie a new color to it by making a knot. Cut off the first color and continue with the new color.
4. Continue until you have almost covered the crossed sticks. Now, wind the yarn around one stick, tying it in a knot so it will not come unfastened. Make a loop for hanging your *ojo de dios*.
5. You may also want to add tassels to the other three arms. To make a tassel, wrap yarn five times around the fingers of one hand. Tie a small piece of yarn through the loop and attach to the arm of the *ojo de dios*. Tie another small piece of yarn around the loop about half an inch (1.3 cm) below the arm. Then cut the bottom of the loop so that it makes a tassel.

An *ojo de dios* decorates your room beautifully. It also makes a lovely gift for a teacher or grown-up.

Easter and *Semana Santa*

Easter, or *Pascua* (PAHS-kwah), is also a religious holiday. The 40 days before Easter are a time for prayer and penance. The week before Easter is called *Semana Santa* (say-MAH-nah SAHN-tah), or Holy Week.

Holy Week marks the time when Christians remember the last days and the death of Jesus. At Easter, they celebrate him as risen from the dead.

During *Semana Santa*, Guatemalans participate in parades and prayers. The parades focus on religious themes. People carry large platforms through the streets. The platforms display scenes from the Bible.

On Good Friday—Friday of *Semana Santa*—large statues of Jesus move through the streets. The procession features Jesus carrying a cross.

People often perform *passion plays* during *Semana Santa*. The plays show the last days of Jesus, from the Last Supper to the Crucifixion. Easter bunnies and eggs, as made popular in the United States, have no place in traditional celebrations of Easter. Here, Easter is a religious holiday.

Semana Santa is also vacation time throughout much of Mexico and Central America. Schools and government offices are all closed. Many families who live in cities head for the beach or the mountains.

Saints' Days

Our Lady of Guadalupe is said to have appeared to Juan Diego in 1531 in Mexico. She is the patron saint of the Americas. She represents the coming together of Native Americans and Europeans. She has brown skin and wears traditional Nahuatl clothing. Her feast day is December 12.

Our Lady of Guadalupe is the same as the Blessed Virgin Mary. The mother of Jesus is honored with many different titles and is seen in many different ways. Our Lady of Suyapa is an important saint in Honduras.

Besides honoring Mary, people also honor the patron saint of their town. They

celebrate saints' days with fiestas and parades, as well as with prayers. Some people feel a religious devotion to the saints. Others just like the celebration.

El Salvador is named for Jesus, who is known as the "savior of the world." *El Salvador* means "the savior." In El Salvador, people celebrate the Feast of the Savior of the World during the first week of August.

Patriotic Holidays

Religious holidays are very important occasions for people in Mexico and Central America and, therefore, often involve much more celebration than patriotic holidays.

Every country celebrates its independence day. For Mexico, that day is September 16. That's when Mexico began its war for independence from Spain. In the small town of Dolores, the church bells rang wildly. Father Hidalgo called the people to revolution: "*¡Viva México! ¡Viva Independencia!*" or "Long Live Mexico! Long Live Independence!" Mexico's war of independence from Spain began in 1810.

Although Mexico won its war of independence, the struggle was not over. In 1861 France invaded Mexico. In 1862 seven thousand French soldiers attacked two forts. Two thousand Mexican soldiers fought back. They won the battle on May 5, which is still celebrated as *Cinco de Mayo* (Fifth of May). Mexican Americans brought the celebration to the United States, and many communities celebrate in various ways. Traditional celebrations always include music and food.

Mexicans also celebrate November 20, the anniversary of the Mexican Revolution of 1910. The revolution was long and bloody. It ended in the triumph of the people over a dictator.

Most of Central America celebrates the same independence day—September 15. In 1821 Spain ruled Guatemala, Honduras, Nicaragua, Costa Rica, and El Salvador. Together, they were called the *Captaincy of Guatemala*. Together, they won their independence from Spain in 1821.

On July 19 Nicaraguans celebrate a revolution. In 1979 the Sandinista revolution threw out a dictator.

Learn a Little Spanish!

Navidad (NAH-vee-dahd): Christmas

Feliz Navidad (fay-LEES NAH-vee-dahd): Merry Christmas

Pascuas (PAHS-kwahs): Easter

Semana Santa (say-MAH-nah SAHN-tah): Holy Week

Día de Independencia (DEE-ah day in-day-pen-DEN-see-ah): Independence Day

Día de la Raza (DEE-ah day lah RAH-sah): Day of the Race, Day of the People

celebrar (sell-ay-BRAHR): to celebrate

fiesta (fee-ESS-tah): celebration or party

Quema del Diablo (KAY-mah dell dee-AH-blow): "Burning the Devil" on the night of December 7

La Gritería (lah gree-tare-EE-ah): the cry or screaming—celebration of the feast of the Blessed Virgin Mary on December 7 in Nicaragua

bombas (BOHM-bahs): fireworks

As part of Colombia, Panama became independent from Spain in 1821. November 28 marks that independence day. Panama remained part of Colombia until 1903. They seceded from Colombia on November 3. November 3 is the official Panamanian independence day.

England ruled Belize as the colony of British Honduras until 1981. Belize celebrates its independence day on September 21. Garifuna Settlement Day, on November 9, celebrates the contributions of Africa to Belize and other Central American countries. St. George's Caye Day, on September 10, celebrates a battle between the British and Spanish for control of Belize.

Millions of people from Mexico and Central America live in the United States today. The next chapter will look at their journeys and some of their stories.

In 2003 immigrants from all across the United States joined in a Freedom Ride to Washington, DC, and New York City. They wanted laws changed to allow family reunification, to guarantee immigrant workers' rights, and to enable them to become citizens more quickly. *Courtesy of Mary C. Turck*

10

La Frontera: Borderlands

This chapter tells stories of people who have come to the United States from Mexico and Central America. Some have risked their lives. Some have lost their lives. Those who now live in the United States add much to its culture.

The river winds for 1,855 miles (2,985 km), through sandy desert and scraggly mesquite bushes. On the north side, they call it the *Río Grande*—the grand river, the big river, the great river. On the south side, it is the *Río Bravo*—the wild river, the strong river, the brave river. The river divides the United States from Mexico.

La Frontera (lah frohn-TEHR-ah), the border, lies on both sides of the Río Grande/Río Bravo. At El Paso/Ciudad Juárez, *La Frontera* leaves the river. From there to the Pacific Ocean, an imaginary line stretches across the desert, marking the boundary between Mexico and the United States. The borderlands lie north and south. They are dry. Usually less than 8 inches (20 cm) of rain falls yearly. Jackrabbits and coyotes travel back and forth across the border. They notice no difference. Two hundred years ago, people crossed the river freely, too.

The Tohono O'odham still cross the border. They are Native Americans. They live on both sides of the border. They always have. They have lived here since before there

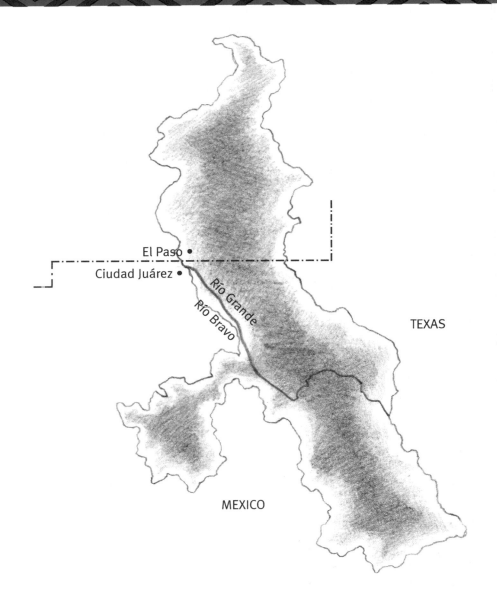

El Paso

Ciudad Juárez

Río Grande

Río Bravo

TEXAS

MEXICO

was a border. They cross back and forth to visit families and to celebrate holidays. United States and Mexican officials let them go. They recognize that the O'odham Nation is older than the border.

For other people, the border stands as a huge, invisible wall. If you are Mexican or Central American, you cannot cross easily. You must prove to the border guards that you have business in the United States. You must convince them that you will return home. Their job is keeping you out.

United States laws make it difficult for immigrants to enter. Many U.S. citizens and lawmakers do not want a lot of people to enter the country. They are afraid that new immigrants will be a burden on the country or will take jobs that citizens now hold.

In order to enter the United States legally, people must have permission from the U.S. government. This permission is shown in special papers or documents. Many come in without legal papers and permission. They are called *undocumented immigrants*. No one knows exactly how many undocumented immigrants live in the United States.

Each year, tens of thousands of people try to cross the Mexico–United States border. They come from Mexico, and from other countries as well. Nicaraguans, Guatemalans, and other Central Americans may walk for weeks to reach the border. Hunger and fear drive them north; danger and death await many.

Every year, hundreds die in the attempt. Some drown in the Río Grande. More die in the desert, victims of the blazing sun. Despite the dangers, people continue to try to enter the land of opportunity because they have no hope for better lives for themselves or their children in their homelands.

The immigrants come for jobs. Juarez is in Mexico, across the river from El Paso, Texas. In Juarez, factory workers earn $1.25 an hour. Across the border, workers earn $5 an hour. Many make more.

Farther to the south, there are no jobs. People move from southern Mexico to Juarez to find work. Some come from Central America. Everyone needs better paying jobs.

The U.S. census counts and classifies people who live in the United States. The

Mexico, of course, is American. So are all the countries of the hemisphere. Mexico, Canada, and the United States are in North America. Belize, Costa Rica, El Salvador, Guatemala, Honduras, Nicaragua, and Panama are in Central America.

2000 census found that one person in eight is "of Hispanic origin." That includes people whose ancestors came from Mexico, Central America, South America, and the Caribbean. Latinos are now the largest minority group in the United States.

About 39 million Latinos live in the United States. About 18 million were born here. Anyone born in the United States is automatically a citizen. Some have lived here for generations.

Two-thirds of Latinos living in the United States come from Mexico. Others have come from Nicaragua, Guatemala, El Salvador, and other Central American countries. Some have come from South America and from Caribbean countries, such as Cuba, Haiti, and the Dominican Republic.

Some Latino residents came to this country recently. About 15 million Latino residents were born outside the United States (census figures vary). Of these, one-quarter have become citizens. Others have legal residence in the United States. Some are undocumented immigrants.

Chicano, Latino, Hispanic

Chicano (chee-CAH-no) means Mexican American. A *Chicano* (male) or *Chicana* (female) identifies with his or her Mexican heritage.

Perhaps her parents came from Mexico. She spoke Spanish before she spoke English. She grew up eating tortillas and beans. She is proud of her Mexican heritage and she is *Chicana*.

Maybe his great-great-grandparents moved to Los Angeles at the turn of the 20th century. He doesn't speak Spanish. He likes hamburgers and hates beans. His mother's ancestors came from Italy, Germany, and France. Still, he is proud of his Mexican heritage and proud to be *Chicano*.

Someone from Nicaragua or Brazil is not *Chicano*. He or she may identify himself or herself as *Latino/Latina*. *Latino* (lah-TEE-no) is a more general term. It means someone who is from some part of Latin America.

Hispanic means Spanish-speaking. Most, but not all, of the countries in Latin America are Spanish-speaking countries. Someone from Mexico can be Chicano, Latino, and Hispanic! People from Spain may be Hispanic, too.

Sometimes people like to identify themselves as *Chicano* or *Latino*. Sometimes they choose to call themselves *Honduran American* or *Guatemalan American*. Respecting other people means letting each person decide how to identify himself or herself.

Most Mexican and Central American immigrants settle in the western United States. They settle in Texas, Arizona, Colorado, New Mexico, or California. Latinos make up almost half the population of Los Angeles.

Some immigrants move on. Latino shops line 18th Street, Division Street, and 26th Street in Chicago. One in four Chicagoans is Latino. Latino workers pick sugar beets and process poultry in Minnesota. Their children attend small-town schools. They drive to Minneapolis and St. Paul to shop in Mexican grocery stores.

Like other immigrant groups, Mexicans and Central Americans enrich the culture of the United States. Latino murals brighten city walls.

Piñatas become Christmas traditions for families whose ancestors came from Poland and Germany. Suburban homes line sidewalks with *luminarias* for holidays and birthdays.

Some families transplant traditions, such as *quinceañeras*. Other traditions, such as Christmas *posadas*, change as they move north. Cultures combine, as potluck dinners see plates of Mexican *tamales* next to Norwegian *lefse* and Vietnamese spring rolls. It is wonderful when cultures mix and people who live near one another and work side by side can also learn from each other.

Immigrant Workers Freedom Ride

In 2003 thousands of people rode buses across the United States to Washington, DC, and New York City. Some were citizens, some were permanent immigrant residents, and a few were people living in the United States without documents. They came from dozens of U.S. cities.

Some of the immigrants came from Latin America. Some came from Africa and Asia. They agreed on four goals. First, they asked that immigrant workers already working hard and paying taxes in the United State be given legal permission to stay there. Second, they asked that immigrants be allowed to become citizens. Third, they

"¡La Migra!"

Alváro Delgado was hanging drywall when they arrived. Suddenly he heard the shouts: "¡La migra! ¡La migra!"—"Immigration! Immigration!" He saw the hundred agents swarming around the construction-site fence. Everywhere, people ran. Delgado hid for hours. Finally, he felt safe enough to come out.

This time *la migra* did not catch him. *La migra* hauled away 125 of his fellow workers. Like him, they were undocumented workers. They did not have legal permission to live in the United States.

Alváro crossed the border when he was 17. That was six years ago. First, he worked in Texas. Then, he moved to Memphis. Now, he works ten-hour days, seven days a week, whenever work is available. He earns $13 an hour. In Mexico, he earned $50 a week. He says he only wants to have a home, car, and money in the bank. He wants to work hard and to enjoy the fruits of his work.

asked for family reunification, so that legal residents could send for children and parents who remained behind in their native countries. Finally, they asked that the legal rights of immigrant workers and of all immigrants be respected. They said:

> Immigrant workers work hard, pay taxes, and sacrifice for their families. They work as construction workers, doctors, nurses, janitors, meat packers, chefs, busboys, engineers, farm workers, and soldiers. They care for our children, tend to our elderly, pick and serve our food, build and clean our houses, and want what we all want: a fair shot at the American Dream.

It's yet to be seen whether this action will make a difference in immigrants' lives. Legislation resulting from the Freedom Ride is still pending.

Ancient Aztecs built the island city of Tenochtitlán. Maya priests and scientists directed the people who built pyramids that have stood for thousands of years.

Nicaraguan poets inspire with their words of love and revolution. Mexican farmers and cooks learned the secrets of corn and chocolate. The people of Mexico and Central America have added rich contributions to the civilization of the world.

Of course, one book cannot begin to describe all of the fascinating history and stories of this part of the world. If you would like to explore further, check out the books, Web pages, movies, museums, and other resources listed in the last section of this book.

Crossing the Border, A Stage Play

Characters

Miguel, smuggler (aka, a coyote). He smuggles immigrants into the United States. He makes good money, but is afraid of being arrested.

José, a father who can't find work in Nuevo Laredo. He has brought his family to the United States in search of a better life. They will do any kind of work, so long as their children can go to school. José carries plastic bags with their belongings.

Maria, a mother, who worked in a *maquila* sewing blue jeans before it closed. She is carrying Juanito in her arms.

Eliza, 10 years old, carries plastic bags with their belongings

Juanito, baby (use a doll wrapped in a blanket for this character)

David, 16 years old, he came from the southern Mexican state of Oaxaca. His family lives in Oaxaca. They raise corn and beans on a small farm. There are no jobs in the rural area. David is their hope. He will find a job in the United States. He will send money back to his family to support them. David carries a plastic bag with his extra clothes.

Teresa, 19 years old, she speaks English and Spanish. She comes from Honduras. She went to school to become a secretary, but there were no jobs available. She hopes that her secretarial and bilingual skills will get her a good job in the United States. Teresa wears a backpack filled with her belongings.

Hector, 43 years old, he left his family in Mexico City. He is a skilled carpenter and plumber, but cannot find work that pays enough to support his family. Hector carries a toolbox.

Tito, early 30s, an immigration officer, carries a walkie-talkie and gun and wears a uniform and badge.

Sam, early 30s, an immigration officer, carries a walkie-talkie and gun and wears a uniform and badge. He is carrying a flashlight with a strong beam.

Props

1 truck, cut out of cardboard
Rocks or benches
2 walkie-talkies
2 toy guns
1 can of soda
1 flashlight, large
Plastic bags full of clothes
Backpack

The stage is dimly lit. It is nighttime. On the right-hand side, two men stand near or lean on the side of a truck. The truck is a cardboard cut-out. On its door, the border patrol logo is painted in bright yellow and blue.

The stage is divided by a river. About two-thirds of the stage lies to the right of the river. Make the river by spreading a long piece of blue fabric down the middle of the stage. The fabric should not be flat or even, but should be crumpled and wavy.

On the left side of the stage, place a few rocks or wooden benches for people to sit on.

As the play opens, the two officers stand next to the truck, or lean against it. Tito sips his can of soda.

Tito: What's that? I hear something moving over there. (points to back of stage)

Sam: (shines flashlight) Ah, that's nothing, just a rabbit. They haven't started coming over yet tonight.

Tito: Yeah, I suppose we still have half an hour before the rush starts. Last night we caught the first bunch about 11.

Sam: I wish we had caught the "coyote" with that bunch. Imagine—just running off and leaving that woman and her kids in the middle of the river!

Tito: Good thing we picked her up anyway. She wouldn't have made it far with three kids.

Sam: I felt sorry for her. She said she didn't have a job or any way to feed the kids.

Tito: Well, they probably got a good breakfast before they were shipped back.

(The two officers freeze in place. Miguel enters, from the left. He seems to be trying to avoid notice, looking back and forth to see if anyone else is there. When he gets to the rock or bench, he turns and motions for people to follow him. The immigrants crowd around him.)

Miguel: Shhhh. We can rest for a little while. We need to cross at about 11 o'clock and it's only 9 now. We are about a mile from the river.

(José and Hector gesture for Maria to sit down with the baby. She sits on the rock, and Eliza sits on the ground next to her. David and Miguel remain standing, and the rest find places to sit on the floor.)

Eliza: How much longer, *Papí*?

José: Just a little while, *mi hija* [my daughter]. Now we rest, before we cross the river.

Eliza: And then we will get a new house?

Maria: In a little while, *mi hija*. We will stay with *Tía* [Aunt] Rosa in her house for a while.

José: *Sí*, I have to find work and get paid before we get our own place.

Hector: What kind of work do you look for?

José: I don't care. I can work in gardens, clean buildings, work in a factory, work in the fields—anything at all.

Hector: That's good. Without papers, you can't get many factory jobs, but there are other kinds of work.

(The group of immigrants freezes in place. Sam and Tito unfreeze.)

Sam: They just keep coming, night after night. Why do they do it?

Tito: Well, my grandfather was one of "them." He crossed in 1942. Never did get his papers.

Sam: What did he do?

Tito: It was easier then. You just needed to work hard. Nobody asked for your papers. So he worked and saved and sent for my grandma. They raised the family in Houston. My dad was born here, in the United States.

Sam: What about your grandpa?

Tito: Oh, he's retired now. Grandma died a few years back, so Grandpa lives with my folks.

Sam: What does he think about your job?

Tito: (laughs) He thinks it's funny. Every time I visit, he yells, "*La migra! Watch out—la migra is here!*"

(Sam laughs, too. Then they freeze in place. The action shifts to the immigrants.)

David: I want to work in the fields. I hear you can make good money following the crops.

Hector: Yeah, you're still young enough to do that. Me—I would rather stay in one place.

Teresa: I want to work in an office. I don't know anything about picking vegetables. I have lived in a city all my life.

Hector: With your good English, you will probably get a job working for some family taking care of their house and kids.

Teresa: But I am a secretary! I finished school, and I know how to use the computer.

Hector: Not much chance of that. You need papers to work in an office. When you apply, you have to show you have legal residence, or they can't hire you.

Teresa (looking frightened, uncertain): I'll find a way to get around it. There has to be a way.

(The group freezes in place.)

Tito: I suppose they still come for the same reasons my grandpa did. To find a job, make a home, raise a family.

Sam: Yeah, but there aren't enough jobs for all the Americans who want one. We can't afford to take in the whole world.

Tito: Well, that's why you and I have these jobs, right—to keep American jobs for Americans.

Sam: Right.

(They freeze in place. The action returns to the immigrants.)

David: Americans don't want to pick strawberries, tomatoes, and asparagus. The work is too hard for them. The pay is too small. That's why I can get a job in the fields. But Americans will work as secretaries.

Hector: Yes—they'll work as carpenters, too. But I will work for less money. So I get odd jobs now and then. And even though I work for less, I still make more than I would in Mexico City. And I can still support my family better by leaving them than by staying with them.

Maria: Is there factory work? I worked in a *maquila*, sewing blue jeans. Only it closed.

Miguel: You need papers to work in a factory. But there are some places that will hire you without papers. You just have to be sure they don't close shop without paying you.

Maria: We are not afraid of hard work. We will find something to do.

Miguel: That's the spirit! Now, let's get going. It's time to cross.

(The immigrants stand up and pick up their bags and backpacks. Eliza takes her father's hand. They stand looking toward the river.)

Sam: Finish up that soda. Time to start moving.

Tito: I'm ready.

(Sam shines the flashlight on the river. Everyone freezes in place.)

Questions for Further Discussion

1. How long ago did your ancestors immigrate to the United States? Where did they come from? Why did they come here? How is this alike or unlike immigrants today?
2. If you were creating U.S. immigration law, who would you let in? Would you let in anyone who really wants to work? People who already have relatives here? People with certain skills, such as doctors, carpenters, and day care workers? Who would you keep out?

Learn a Little Spanish!

ciudadano (see-oo-dah-DAH-no): citizen
frontera (frohn-TEHR-ah): frontier, border
coyote (coy-OH-tay): a wild animal; also a smuggler who is paid to take people across the border
migra (MEE-grah): immigration, immigration police
inmigrante (een-mee-GRAHN-tay): immigrant
policía (poh-lee-SEE-ah): police
trabajo (trah-BAH-ho): work
libertad (lee-behr-TAHD): freedom, liberty
país (pie EES): country

Resources

For Further Exploration

Chapter 1: Ancient Roots

Books

Garland, Sherry. *Indio*. New York: Harcourt Brace & Company, 1995.
Fourteen-year-old Ipa-tah-chi is captured by raiding Spaniards and sold into slavery. (For junior high and older.)

Rockwell, Anne F. *The Boy Who Wouldn't Obey: A Mayan Legend*. New York: Greenwillow Books, 2000.
Anne Rockwell adapts a Maya legend about a disobedient boy taken as a servant by the mighty god, Chac. The illustrations are based on images found on ceramic vessels surviving from the ancient Mayas.

Shetterly, Susan Hand. *The Dwarf Wizard of Uxmal*. New York: Atheneum, 1990.
A Yucatan Maya legend tells about a magical boy hatched from an egg and guarded by a snake and an old woman. The boy grows up to become a wise king of Uxmal.

Wood, Frances M. *Daughter of Madrugada*. New York: Random House, 2002.
In 1846, Cesa lives in Mexico—but then the United States takes the land. How will her life change?

Zubizarreta, Rosalma, Harriet Rohmer, and David Schecter. *The Woman Who Outshone the Sun/La mujer que brillaba aún más que el sol*. With illustrations by Fernando Olivera. San Francisco, CA: Children's Book Press, 1991.
This wonderful legend is part of the oral history of the Zapotec Indians of Oaxaca, Mexico. Alejandro Cruz Martinez retold it as a poem, and his poem inspired this book. Read the story of a beautiful woman who is mistreated because she is different, but nonetheless teaches people kindness and forgiveness. (In Spanish and in English.)

Web Sites

Día de la Raza
www.elbalero.gob.mx/kids/about/html/holidays/race_kids.html
This site, sponsored by the government of Mexico, describes the reasons for celebrating *La Día de la Raza* on October 12.

Lost King of the Maya
www.pbs.org/wgbh/nova/maya/
Visit Nova on-line to learn more about the Maya city of Copán, Maya hieroglyphics, and Maya kings. Complete with teacher's guide, maps, and activities.

Mexican Culture Taught Through the Aztec Calendar
www.yale.edu/ynhti/curriculum/units/1985/6/85.06.02.x.html#i
Great resource for teachers! Produced by the Yale-New Haven Teachers' Institute, this site includes not only the pronunciation guide used in this book, but also lesson plans, legends, and much more!

Chapter 2: Country by Country

Books

Cameron, Ann. *Colibrí*. New York: Farrar, Straus, Giroux, 2003.
A four-year-old girl is snatched from her parents on a crowded bus. For eight years, she travels the countryside with the man she knows as "Uncle." She still remembers her parents and longs for them, but will she ever find them?

Foley, Erin. *Cultures of the World: Costa Rica*. New York: Marshall Cavendish, 1997.

McGaffey, Leta. *Cultures of the World: Honduras*. New York: Marshall Cavendish, 1999.

Mike, Jan M. *Opossum and the Great Firemaker*. Mahway, NJ: Troll Associates, 1993.
A Mexican legend tells how Iguana stole fire and how Opossum brought fire back to earth.

Palacios, Argentina. *The Hummingbird King*. Mahway, NJ: Troll Associates. 1993.
Retelling of Guatemalan legend of a young prince who is murdered by his uncle and becomes the quetzal bird—the symbol of Guatemala.

Web Sites

Belize Tourism Board
www.travelbelize.org/cult.html
   Photos and information show the beauty of
   Belize.
Cloudforest Alive!
www.cloudforestalive.org
   Take an electronic field trip to Costa Rica
   with this fascinating Web site!
Honduran Embassy
www.hondurasemb.org/geography.htm
   Here's a lesson on Honduran geography.
Peace Corps Lesson Plans
www.peacecorps.gov/wws/guides/Honduras/
   honduras4.html
   These lesson plans include letters and reflec-
   tions from Peace Corps volunteers in
   Honduras—very interesting!
Rainforest Science
www.pbs.org/tal/costa_rica/index.html
   Take an electronic field trip to Costa Rica
   with this fascinating Web site!
World Flag Database
   www.flags.net/indexp.htm
   Here you can see the flags in full color.

Chapter 3: Life Above the Clouds

Books

Argueta, Jorge. *Zipitio*. Toronto: Groundwood
   Books, 2003.
   A Salvadoran story, based on the Pipil legend
   of the Zipitio, a man older than the river but
   only as tall as a child, who falls in love with all
   the young girls in the village as they grow up.
Argueta, Manlio. *Magic Dogs of the Volcanoes/Los
   perros mágicos de los volcanes*. With illustrations
   by Elly Simmons. San Francisco, CA:
   Children's Book Press, 1990.
   In El Salvador, magic dogs called *conejos* have
   been the subjects of many traditional folktales.
   An acclaimed Salvadoran author presents his
   original, contemporary folktale about these
   animals. (In Spanish and in English.)
Silverstone, Michael, and Charlotte Bunch.
   *Rigoberta Menchu: Defending Human Rights in
   Guatemala*. New York: Feminist Press at
   CUNY, 1999.
   Discusses the life of the Nobel Peace Prize-
   winning Guatemalan woman who began life
   in the mountains and moved on to the world.

Web Sites

Cerro Negro
www.volcanoworld.org/vwdocs/volc_images/
   south_america/cerro_negro.html
   Brilliant photographs accompany a scientist's
   journal of Nicaragua's Cerro Negro Volcano
   activity.
How to Make Kites
www.kirkwood.cc.ia.us/esl/kites.htm
   Virginia Aspuac tells how she and her brothers
   made kites in Guatemala.
Journey North
www.learner.org/jnorth/
   Journey North traces the migration of
   monarch butterflies from Mexico to the
   United States and Canada and back again—
   a lot of stories from schools and students at
   both ends of the journey, great pictures,
   activities for schools and classes.

Chapter 4: On the Atlantic Coast

Books

Rohmer, Harriet, and Dorminster Wilson.
   *Mother Scorpion Country/La tierra de la
   madre escorpión*. With illustrations by
   Virginia Stearns. San Francisco, CA:
   Children's Book Press, 1987.
   From the Miskito people of Nicaragua's
   Atlantic Coast, this book tells the legend of
   a young man who accompanies his beloved
   wife to Mother Scorpion Country, which is
   beyond the land of the living. (In Spanish
   and in English.)
Rohmer, Harriet, and James de Sauza. *Brother
   Anansi and the Cattle Ranch/El Hermano
   Anansi y el Rancho de Ganado*. San
   Francisco, CA: Children's Book Press, 1989.
   (In Spanish and in English.)

Web Sites

Garinet Global
www.garinet.com
    A site all about Garifuna people today.
Kriol (Creole) Language
www.kriol.org.bz/LanguagePages/Language_
    Dictionary.htm
    For a mini-dictionary of the Creole language
    spoken in Belize, explore this Web site.
San Blas de Cuna Islands
http://Park.org/SanBlasDeCuna/home.html
    Tour the islands where the Cuna people live
    and visit a *mola* gallery.

Chapter 5: Going to School

Books

Alessio, Carolyn, ed. *The Voices of Hope/Las Voces
    de La Esperanza.* Carbondale, IL: Southern
    Illinois University Press, 2003.
    Poems, stories, and drawings by the children
    of La Esperanza, Guatemala.
Velásquez, Gloria. *Juanita Fights the School
    Board.* Houston, TX: Arte Público, 1994.
    Roosevelt High expels Juanita after she
    fights with a girl who slanders her family.
    When Juanita confronts the school board,
    she proves that fairness should triumph over
    race and class differences. This is the first in
    the Roosevelt High School series, which

offers characters that adolescents can relate
to set in a multicultural high school.

Web Sites

Peace Corps Lesson Plans
www.peacecorps.gov/wws/guides/honduras/
    (For a description of this site, see listing
    under Chapter 2.)
Mexico for Kids
www.elbalero.gob.mx/index_kids.html
    The Mexican government welcomes you to
    history, exploration, games, and more!
550 Books for Nicaragua
www.mn-leon.org/550Books.html
    This sister city project is building mobile
    libraries for Nicaraguan teachers and students.

Chapter 6: Art and Poetry

Books

Ancona, George. *Murals: Walls that Sing.* New
    York: Marshall Cavendish, 2003.
    This lavishly illustrated book of Mexican
    and U.S. neighborhood murals will inspire
    young artists to decorate their own commu-
    nities.
Cruz, Bárbara. *Rubén Blades: Salsa Singer and
    Social Activist.* Springfield, NJ: Enslow
    Publishers, 1997.
    Biography of a Panamanian American
    musician and actor who returned to Panama

to run for president and work for the
environment.
Volkmer, Jane. *Song of the Chirinmia/La Musica
    de la Chirimia.* Minneapolis, MN:
    Carolrhoda Books. 1990.
    A Guatemalan folktale tells how a young
    prince learned music from the quetzal bird
    and made the first flute. (In Spanish and in
    English.)

Web Sites

Cyber Anthology of Nicaraguan Poetry
www.nicapoets.org/cyber-anthology/cyber-
    anth.html
    If you'd like to read more about Nicaraguan
    poets, or to read some of their poetry, this is
    a good place to begin.
Frida Kahlo
    www.fridakahlo.it
    Meet artist Frida Kahlo through her paint-
    ings, biography, and more.
Mexico: Splendors of Thirty Centuries
www.humanities-interactive.org/splendors/
    An online museum, curriculum, and
    teacher's guide.
The Virtual Diego Rivera Web Museum
www.diegorivera.com
    See Diego Rivera's magnificent paintings
    and murals in an online museum!

Chapter 7: Daily Grind: Corn and Coffee

Books

Castaneda, Omar S. *Abuela's Weave*. New York: Lee & Low Books, 1993.
> In a story about everyday life in Guatemala, *Abuela* (Grandma) teaches Esperanza how to weave, while Esperanza helps *Abuela* sell her weaving.

Cohn, Diana. *Sí, Se Puede!/Yes, We Can! Janitor Strike in L.A.* With illustrations by Francisco Delgado. El Paso, TX: Cinco Puntos Press, 2002.
> An inspiring story about the janitors' strike in Los Angeles. Carlitos' *mamá* is very active in the strike because she wants to be able to take better care of Carlito and his grandmother. Carlito decides to help by carrying a sign he has made that says, "I Love My Mamá. She is a janitor!" Though this story is set in the United States, it introduces union organizing to children. (In Spanish and in English.)

Gerson, Mary-Joan. *People of Corn*. Boston, MA: Little, Brown & Co, 1995.
> A vivid retelling of the Maya creation story in which the gods make the first people from corn, this shows the importance of corn in Maya culture.

Web Sites

Cloudforest Initiatives
www.hwpics.com/cloudforest-mexico/interview_with_lucio_gonzalez.htm
> Lucio Gonsalez tells the story of his organic coffee cooperative, describing how it was formed and what he and his fellow members do.

In Their Own Words
www.uniteunion.org/sweatshops/guess/mexico/mexico5.html
> Read more about *maquiladoras* in Mexico, including lots of interviews with workers.

Maquila Solidarity Network
www.maquilasolidarity.org
> Canadians organizing to help *maquila* workers provide useful information and ways to get involved.

U.S. Labor Education in the Americas Project
www.usleap.org
> A site with information on *maquilas* and suggestions for how to take action.

Chapter 8: Celebrating Life

Books

Chambers, Veronica. *Marisol and Magdalena*. New York: Hyperion Books for Children, 1998.
> Two best friends living in Brooklyn both come from families steeped in their Panamanian cultural roots. When one is sent to spend a year with her grandmother in Panama, the story explores the colorful threads of dual heritage as the girls journey toward womanhood.

———. *Quinceañera Means Sweet Fifteen*. New York: Hyperion Books for Children, 2001.
> In the vibrant sequel to *Marisol and Magdalena*, the two girls team up again in preparation for their *quinceañeras*, or fifteenth-birthday celebrations. The teens face issues ranging from friendship and family turmoil to growing up in a single-parent home.

Garza, Carmen Lomas. *Family Pictures/Cuadros de familia*. San Francisco, CA: Children's Book Press, 1990.
> Stories and paintings of the author's family and growing up on the Texas–Mexico border. (In Spanish and in English.)

———. *In My Family/En Mi Familia*. San Francisco, CA: Children's Book Press, 1996.
> These stories tell of growing up, daily life, and family celebrations and traditions on the Texas–Mexico border. (In Spanish and in English.)

Video

Sweet 15
Produced by Wonderworks.
> A Mexican American girl comes of age in Los Angeles, facing the difficulties of growing up and celebrating her *quinceañera*.

Web Sites

A Great Little Nicaraguan Wedding
www.guidenicaragua.com/newsletter/update
_nicaraguaMay2003.shtml
The author tells about his wedding in a
small Nicaraguan town—with pictures!

Chapter 9: Religious and Patriotic Holidays

Books

Harris, Zoe, and Suzanne Williams. *Piñatas and Smiling Skeletons*. Berkeley, CA: Pacific View Press, 1998.
Background, legends, recipes, crafts, and celebrations of a year of special Mexican festivals, including: the Virgin of Guadalupe, Carnaval, Corpus Christi, Independence Day, and *El Día de los Muertos*.

Web Sites

La Purisima
www.guidenicaragua.com/newsletter/update_
nicaraguaDec2002.shtml
Direct from León, a story of the December 7th celebration of *La Gritería*.

Chapter 10: La Frontera: Borderlands

Books

Ada, Alma Flor. *I Love Saturdays y Domingos*. New York: Atheneum Books for Young Readers, 2002.
A charming account of how a young girl's Saturdays with her English-speaking grandma and grandpa and *Domingos* (Sundays) with her Spanish-speaking *abuelito* and *abuelita* help her acknowledge and take pride in both parts of her ethnicity. (Written in English, spiced with Spanish.)
Atkin, S. Beth. *Voices from the Fields: Children of Migrant Farmworkers Tell Their Stories*. Boston, MA: Little, Brown & Co., 1993.
Evocative black-and-white photographs, poems, and first-person interviews offer readers a glimpse of the lives of migrant farmworker children by showing the diversity of migrant family situations.
Buss, Fran Leeper. *Journey of the Sparrows*. New York: Puffin Books, 1991.
Mexican immigrants stow away in a truck to travel across the border and north to Chicago.
Cisneros, Sandra. *The House on Mango Street*. New York: Vintage Books, 1991.
Young Esperanza Cordero wants more than the world offers her in inner-city Chicago. A touching story of a young girl discovering the hard realities of life, coming into her own power, and deciding for herself what she will become. (Also available in Spanish as *La Casa en Mango Street*. Suggested for ages 12 and older.)
Ryan, Pam Muñoz. *Esperanza Rising*. New York: Scholastic, 2000.
Esperanza and her mother are forced to leave their life of wealth and privilege in Mexico to go work in the labor camps of southern California, where they must adapt to the harsh circumstances facing Mexican farm workers on the eve of the Great Depression. (Also available in Spanish as *Esperanza Renace*.)
Soto, Gary. *Cesar Chavez: A Hero for Everyone*. New York: Simon & Schuster, 2003.
Biography of the Mexican American leader of the United Farm Workers.

Video

Maricela
Produced by Wonderworks.
Maricela is a young Salvadoran refugee who faces issues of culture clash and friendship in Los Angeles.

Web Sites

Beyond the Border
www.pbs.org/itvs/beyondtheborder/index.html

PBS traces the stories of four brothers who leave their home in Mexico to follow the dream of a better life in the United States.

Coalition of Immokalee Workers
www.ciw-online.org
Migrant workers in Florida organize to get basic rights.

National Immigration Forum
www.immigrationforum.org
Track immigration news and laws and find out how to write to Congress about immigration policies.

Museums

The Smithsonian Institution is the national museum of the United States, with multiple focuses and locations in Washington, DC. Supporters of a National Museum of the American Latino want the Smithsonian to build and administer this museum to honor the cultures of the nation's largest minority group. Until that happens, many museums scattered across the country provide homes for Latino art, history, and culture.

California

Galería de la Raza
2857 24th Street
San Francisco, CA 94110
(415) 826-8009
www.galeriadelaraza.org

The *galería* was founded by Latino-rights activists. Through art exhibitions, multimedia presentations, performances and spoken-word events, screenings, computer-generated murals, and educational activities, the *galería* addresses issues confronting Latino peoples, such as immigration policy, violence, war, family life, spirituality, and race politics.

Mexican Heritage Plaza
1700 Alum Rock Avenue
San José, CA 95116
1-800-MHC-VIVA
www.mhcviva.org

The Mexican Heritage Plaza hosts the San José International Mariachi Festival and Conference every July, with *mariachi* concerts, a *mariachi* Mass, and an outdoor *mariachi* festival.

Museum of Latin American Art (MoLAA)
628 Alamitos Avenue
Long Beach, CA 90802
(562) 437-1689
www.molaa.com/inform.asp

Contemporary Latin American art—art created since World War II—is the focus of this museum. It also features a restaurant with Latin American cuisine and a museum store.

Colorado

Museo de las Américas
861 Santa Fe Drive
Denver, CO 80204
(303) 571-4401
www.museo.org/museo-information.html

Dedicated to educating the public about the artistic and cultural achievements of Latinos in the Americas, the *museo* is located in the heart of Denver's Latino community. Its exhibitions range from pre-Columbian to Spanish Colonial to modern.

Illinois

The Mexican Fine Arts Center Museum of Chicago
1852 W. 19th Street
Chicago, IL 60608
(312) 738-1503
www.mfacmchicago.org

Since the museum opened in 1987, it has grown to become the largest Mexican or Latino arts institution in the country. The museum also operates Radio Arte, a bilingual, youth-operated radio station that trains young people from ages 15 to 21.

Nebraska

El Museo Latino
4701 S. 25th Street
Omaha, Nebraska 68107
(402) 731-1137

www.omaha.org/oma/latino.htm

As the first Latino museum in Nebraska, El Museo Latino's focus is on the art of Latin peoples from all the Americas.

New Mexico

El Rancho de las Golondrinas
334 Los Pinos Road
Santa Fe, NM 87507
(505) 471-2261
www.golondrinas.org/about.html

The "Ranch of the Swallows" is a living history museum dedicated to the heritage and culture of Spanish Colonial New Mexico, with original buildings dating from the early 18th century. Staff dresses in old-time styles to show how life was lived then.

National Hispanic Cultural Center
1701 4th Street SW
Albuquerque, NM 87102
(505) 246-2261

www.nhccnm.org

The museum's mission is "preserve, interpret, and showcase Hispanic arts and lifeways" through visual, performing, media, and culinary arts.

New York

El Museo del Barrio
1230 Fifth Avenue at 104th Street
New York, NY 10029
(212) 831-7272
www.elmuseo.org

El Museo del Barrio began in 1969 with a focus on Puerto Rican culture, and it has since expanded to represent all of Latin America and the Caribbean.

Texas

Guadalupe Cultural Arts Center
1300 Guadalupe Street
San Antonio, TX 78207

www.guadalupeculturalarts.org

The Guadalupe Cultural Arts Center is more than a museum, offering dance, literature, media arts, theater arts, visual arts, and music events. Its focus is on Chicano/Latino/Native American arts and culture.

The Jack S. Blanton Museum of Art
The University of Texas at Austin
23rd & San Jacinto
Austin, TX 78712
(512) 471-7324
www.blantonmuseum.org

The Blanton Museum has a Latin American gallery with 1,600 works of art, representing over 500 artists from 18 countries.

The Museo Americano will open in San Antonio, Texas, in 2004–2005, with a promise to tell the social and cultural history of the Latino experience in America. For more information on this museum, go to www.thealameda.org.

Holidays and Celebrations

January

1: New Year's Day/New Year's Eve

6: *Día de Los Reyes Magos* (Day of the Three Kings)

This day is even more important than Christmas in much of Latin America. In religious tradition, January 6 marks the day that three kings came to see the baby Jesus, bearing gifts. Many families exchange gifts on this day.

March

9: Baron Bliss Day

Celebrated in Belize, in honor of an English nobleman who visited Belize in the 1920s and left his fortune to Belize.

21: Benito Juárez birthday

Benito Juárez was one of Mexico's most beloved presidents.

31: César Chávez birthday

California, Arizona, and Texas have made the day a state holiday honoring the Mexican American labor and civil-rights leader.

April

Easter and *La Semana Santa* (Holy Week)

These vary from year to year since the dates are set according to the lunar calendar.

May

5: *Cinco de Mayo* (Fifth of May)

Marks the victory of the Mexican army over French invaders in the Battle of Puebla.

10: *Día de Las Madres* (Day of the Mothers)
Mexican Mother's Day.

July

19: Nicaragua's Liberation Day

Marks the 1979 victory of the Sandinista revolution.

August

1–6: Feast of *El Salvador del Mundo* (Savior of the World)

Honors the patron saint of El Salvador.

September

15: Independence Day for El Salvador, Costa Rica, Guatemala, Honduras, and Nicaragua

16: Mexican Independence Day

On this day, Father Miguel Hidalgo called Mexicans to begin the fight for independence from Spain.

21: Belize Independence Day

October

12: *Día de la Raza* (Day of Our Race)

November

1–2: *Los Días de los Muertos* (Days of the Dead)

9: Belize's Garifuna Settlement Day

20: Mexican anniversary of the Revolution of 1910

28: Panama's Independence Day

December

7–8: *La Purísima* , Nicaragua's celebration honoring the mother of Jesus.

12: *Día de la Virgen de Guadalupe*, the feast day of Our Lady of Guadalupe.

16–24: *Las Posadas*

24 and 25: *La Nochebuena y La Navidad* (Christmas Eve and Christmas)

Teachers' Guide

Activities by Grade Level

Some of the activities in this book can be enjoyed by all ages, but others work better for children with a certain level of manual dexterity. Some activities are individual and others work well in groups. This Teachers' Guide will help you to go right to the activities that will work best in your classroom.

The activities recommended for each grade level do not include cooking activities. These work well at home, but few classrooms are equipped for food preparation. In general, the activities recommended for classrooms require inexpensive, readily available materials and can be completed in a relatively short time.

Each stage play deals with significant social and personal issues. As a teacher, you will want to read the material in the chapter and be prepared to discuss these issues as your class prepares the drama. The plays will require more class time and preparation than other activities.

Early Elementary (K through Second Grade)

Activity: Yarn Painting, p. 60
You may want to adapt this activity by furnishing pre-printed picture outlines for students to "paint" with yarn.

Activity: Creating an Alfombra, p. 119
For young students, substitute confetti-sized scraps of colored paper for sand. Whoever cleans the classroom floors will be grateful! This is a good activity for group work. Once students have agreed on (or been given) a large design, a small group can collaborate in gluing the pieces

in place. Glue sticks will work better than liquid glue.

Activity: Ojo de Dios, p. 123
Simplify this activity for younger students by taping the craft sticks together before they begin winding the yarn.

Activity: Papel Picado, p. 105
Third and Fourth Grade
Read sections of the book aloud to explain the background for each activity.

Activity: Creating an Aztec Calendar, p. 8
This is a good group activity. A small group can collaborate on a calendar. Or the whole class can work together, with two or three students working together on each month.

Activity: Writing with Hieroglyphics and Making a Name for Yourself, p. 10
Challenge students to read each other's names or to come up with different ways to represent the name of the school or the school mascot.

Activity: Making Music with Drums, Maracas, Güiros, and Claves, p. 50
Check the library for Garifuna or Afro-Caribbean music to play while students work.

Activity: Painting a Mural, p. 73
Students can work together to create related sections of a mural that will cover a wall of the classroom or be displayed outside the classroom in the hallway.

Activity: The Tree of Life, p. 78

Activity: Creating an Ofrenda, p. 80

Activity: Painting in the Salvadoran Style, p. 41

Activity: Carving, p. 36

Fifth and Sixth Grade

Fifth and sixth graders typically think they know quite a lot. They are ready for more complex activities, and especially ready for dramatic presentations.

Activity: Writing with Hieroglyphics and Making a Name for Yourself, p. 10
Challenge students to read each other's names or to come up with different ways to represent the name of the school or the school mascot.

Activity: Painting in the Salvadoran Style, p. 41
Give students a single subject to paint and have them paint it in two different styles. For example, they might paint birds in a tree, first using the Salvadoran style and then painting in an Impressionist style.

Activity: Creating an Ofrenda, p. 80

Activity: Carving, p. 36
A class can stage an exhibit of soap carvings or *ofrendas* for the whole school.

Activity: Capirucho, p. 60
Expand this activity by arranging recess or noon-hour tournaments.

Activity: *La Huelga* (The Strike), A Stage Play, p. 65

Activity: *The Union*, A Stage Play, p. 98

Activity: Crossing the Border, A Stage Play, p. 133

Junior High-School Students

Activity: Capirucho, p. 60
Expand this activity by arranging recess or noon-hour tournaments.

Activity: Painting a Mural, p. 73
If you have a hallway or community space that they can decorate, junior high students can rise to the challenge of designing and painting a real mural.

Activity: Political Puppets, p. 82

Activity: *La Huelga* (The Strike), A Stage Play, p. 65

Activity: *The Union*, A Stage Play p. 98

Activity: *Crossing the Border*, A Stage Play, p. 133

Additional Resources for Teachers

Merrill, Yvonne Y. *Hands-On Latin America: Art Activities for All Ages.* Salt Lake City, UT: Kits Publishing, 1997.
    Beautiful photography and lots of craft ideas.
Milord, Susan. *Mexico: 40 Activities to Experience Mexico Past and Present.* Charlotte, VT: Williamson Publishing. 1999.
    Lively introduction to various aspects of Mexican history and life today.
Ruiz, Octavio, Amy Sanders, and Meredith Sommers. *Many Faces of Mexico.* Minneapolis, MN: Resource Center of the Americas, 1998.
    Interdisciplinary curriculum for teaching and learning about contemporary Mexico and Mexican history. Contains background information, primary-source materials, lesson plans, student worksheets, and dozens of activities for the classroom.
Vigil, Angel. *Una Linda Raza: Cultural and Artistic Traditions of the Hispanic Southwest.* Golden, CO: Fulcrum Publishing. 1998.
    Wonderful introduction to Mexican and Mexican American traditions and history.

History Standards and Learning Objectives

The activities and information in *Mexico and Central America* can be used in the classroom to support learning history standards. The development of the history standards was administered by the National Center for History in the Schools at the University of California, Los Angeles, under the guidance of the National Council for History Standards. The standards were developed with funding from the National Endowment for the Humanities and the U.S. Department of Education for Grades K–4 and 5–12, in particular:

History Standards for Grades K-4

Topic 1:	Living and Working Together in Families and Communities, Now and Long Ago
Standard 1	Family life now and in the recent past; family life in various places long ago.
Standard 1B	The student understands the different ways of life of people of diverse racial, religious, and ethnic groups, and how various national origins have transmitted their beliefs and values.
Topic 4:	The History of Peoples of Many Cultures Around the World
Standard 7	Selected attributes and historical developments of various societies in Africa, the Americas, Asia, and Europe.

World History Standards for Grades 5-12

Era 3	Classical Traditions, Major Religions, and Giant Empires, 1000 B.C.E.–300 C.E.
Standard 4	The development of early agrarian civilizations in Mesoamerica.

United States History Standards for Grades 5-12

Era 1	Three Worlds Meet (Beginnings to 1620 C.E.)
Standard 1	Comparative characteristics of societies in the Americas, Western Europe, and Western Africa that increasingly interacted after 1450.
Era 10	Contemporary United States (1968 to the present)
Standard 1	Recent developments in foreign and domestic politics.
Standard 2	Economic, social, and cultural developments in contemporary United States.

Index

Other Books from Chicago Review Press

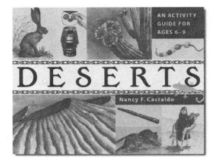

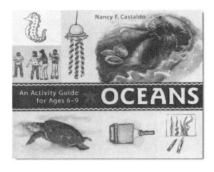

The Civil Rights Movement for Kids
A History with 21 Activities
By Mary C. Turck

"This is a much-needed work that should be in every school and public library, as well as in the home."

—Myrlie Evers-Williams, Chairman Emeritus, NAACP

"It is wonderful to see such a comprehensive guide to civil rights education for young people."

—Kweisi Mfume, president, NAACP

Hands-on activities include sharing a freedom feast with friends, conducting an attitudes-on-race survey, singing freedom songs, hosting a film festival, learning how to campaign for human rights, and more.

Ages 9 & up
Illustrated throughout
$14.95 (CAN $22.95) 1-55652-370-X

Deserts
An Activity Guide for Ages 6–9
By Nancy F. Castaldo

Introducing children to the wild and often misunderstood environment of the desert and the people and cultures that thrive in and around them. Filled with engaging activities and ideas on how children can help protect these delicate environments.

Illustrated throughout
$14.95 (CAN $22.95) 1-55652-524-9

Oceans
An Activity Guide for Ages 6–9
By Nancy F. Castaldo
*A selection of the Primary Teacher's Book Club

"Using fun activities and games, *Oceans* brilliantly underscores the connection that kids have with the oceans."

—Barbara Jeanne Polo, executive director, American Oceans Campaign

Illustrated throughout
$14.95 (CAN $22.95) 1-55652-443-9

Rainforests
An Activity Guide for Ages 6–9
By Nancy F. Castaldo

Rainforest-inspired activities introduce children to plants, animals, and people that contribute to the beauty of these forests, and encourage young readers to become active defenders of the rainforests no matter where they live.

Illustrated throughout
$14.95 (CAN $22.95) 1-55652-476-5

Available at your favorite bookstore or by calling (800) 888-4741.
www.chicagoreviewpress.com

CHICAGO REVIEW PRESS

Distributed by Independent Publishers Group
www.ipgbook.com